GUILFORD COURTHOUSE

BATTLEGROUND AMERICA GUIDES offer a unique approach to the battles and battlefields of America. Each book in the series highlights a small American battlefield—sometimes a small portion of a much larger battlefield. All of the units, important individuals, and actions of each engagement on the battlefield are described in a clear and concise narrative. Detailed maps complement the text and illustrate small unit action at each stage of the battle. Historical images and modern-day photographs tie the dramatic events of the past to today's battlefield site and highlight the importance of terrain in battle. The present-day battlefield is described in detail with suggestions for touring the site.

GUILFORD COURTHOUSE

Nathanael Greene's Victory in Defeat
March 15, 1781

John Hairr

DA CAPO PRESS
A Member of the Perseus Books Group

Many thanks to Theodore P. Savas for creating the maps and making a substantial contribution to the narrative text of this book.

Published by Da Capo Press
A Member of the Perseus Books Group
http://www.dacapopress.com

Typeset and designed by K & P Publishing
Maps by Theodore P. Savas

Cataloging-in-Publication data for this book is available from the Library of Congress.

ISBN 0-306-81171-5

Da Capo Press books are available at special discounts for bulk purchases in the U.S. by corporations, institutions, and other organizations. For more information, please contact the Special Markets Department at the Perseus Books Group, 11 Cambridge Center, Cambridge, MA 02142, or call (617) 252-5298.

First edition, first printing.

1 2 3 4 5 6 7 8 9—05 04 03 02

Printed and Bound in the United States of America.

CONTENTS

INTRODUCTION

The battle of Guilford Courthouse was fought March 15, 1781, near a small crossroads village in what was then the back country of North Carolina. Today, the battlefield sits in the northern edge of the sprawling city of Greensboro. Fortunately, much of the battlefield was preserved by a group of farsighted individuals in the late nineteenth century.

As the site of the largest land battle fought in North Carolina during the American Revolution, Guilford Courthouse National Military Park is a popular destination for those seeking to learn more about the state's history. As this book will show, the battle was the culminating combat in a two-month campaign that began on the Catawba River in southwestern North Carolina in January of 1781. General Nathanael Greene proved able enough to outrun and outmaneuver the British army under Lord Charles Cornwallis, buying time to strengthen his army so that his men might be a match for their better-trained and more disciplined adversaries.

Hindsight has convinced most historians that Guilford Courthouse was the pivotal event that led ultimately to the surrender of the British Army at Yorktown, Virginia, in October of 1781. Prevailing wisdom seems to be that Cornwallis's army was so badly mauled at Guilford Courthouse and left in such logistical straits that he was forced to scamper to the coast and seek protection from the garrison at Wilmington. Later, he appears on the shores of the James River in Virginia, cowering behind the trenches of Yorktown waiting to be rescued from the hands of General George Washington and the Continental Army, which had marched south to finish off what was left of Cornwallis's command. Perhaps this is so.

There is, however, another side of the story. When the British left Guilford, they were marching for much needed supplies and reinforcements at Cross Creek, North Carolina, an important inland port on the Cape Fear River. These materials were unavailable at Cross Creek, forcing a disappointed Cornwallis to continue all the way to the supply base at Wilmington. During this time he continued to tell the inhabitants of North Carolina and his men that he would return to Hillsboro in the summer and renew the liberation of the province. He firmly believed that at the time.

Several individuals were dispatched by Cornwallis and his subordinates into the central portion of the state to organize the Loyalists for the coming campaign. The successes of several of these bands during the next year, most notably the one led by Colonel David Fanning, hint at what might have come to pass had Cornwallis kept his promise and returned to the central portion of North Carolina to prosecute the war against the Whigs. But the Tories who went to their homes thinking the British government was about to finally make good on its promise of support were in for a rude awakening.

Fully rested, resupplied, and reorganized, Cornwallis changed his mind and decided to shift the campaign north into Virginia to knock out the source of so much of Greene's supplies and reinforcements. He set out from Wilmington in April of 1781 and headed north for a junction with another contingent of British forces under General Benedict Arnold. The British enjoyed modest success in their campaign in Virginia during the summer of 1781. But ignorance of the local terrain allowed Cornwallis to be pinned down in the trenches at Yorktown, where he and his men hunkered down to await the arrival of the British fleet that would lift the siege and provide a way out of the Chesapeake. Help did not arrive, and the British navy was unable to break through a French blockade during a brief sea battle off the mouth of Chesapeake Bay. The British ships had been in tropical waters far too long, and their wooden ships had been eaten out from under them by parasitical mollusks and worms. The fleet sailed north, intending to come back and break through the French blockade shortly after repairs were undertaken. They had no idea of the gravity of Cornwallis's situation, and the fleet did not return until after the British at Yorktown had surrendered. The lowly teredo worm, perhaps more so than the battle with General Greene that spring, doomed Cornwallis and his troops.

The hard-earned and expensive victory that the British soldiers won over the Continentals and militia at Guilford Courthouse should have earned them a place in the annals of British military history. Instead, political opponents of the war back home in England seized upon the casualties suffered and held them up as an example of why Britain should get out of the war. Many, though, appreciated the achievements of the king's forces at Guilford Courthouse. One of these was the perceptive Colonel Charles Stedman, who was present during the battle. He later compared the victory to some of the most notable military achievements in the history of Great Britain. "History, perhaps, does not furnish an instance of a battle gained under all the disadvantages which the British troops, assisted by a regiment of Hessians and some yagers, had to contend against at Guilford Court-house," wrote Stedman. "Nor is there, perhaps, on the records of history, an instance of a battle fought with more determined perseverance than was shown by the British troops on that memorable day. The battle of Crecy, of Poitiers, and of Agincourt, the glory of our own country, and the admiration of ages, had in each of them, either from a particular local situation, or other fortunate and favorable circumstances, something in a degree to counter-balance the disparity in numbers. Here time, place and numbers, all united against the British."

Ironically, the battle of Guilford Courthouse is best remembered as the first in a series of tactical military defeats suffered by General Nathanael Greene, each of which ultimately wore down the British army in the south, leading to victory for the colonies in the struggle for independence from Great Britain.

Perhaps the true importance of the battle is not who won or lost on that cold and wet day back in March of 1781. Guilford Courthouse was the culminating point of an arduous campaign in which General Greene learned the true worth of his men, and his men learned the true worth of their leader. Without this confidence, the southern army would never have been able to withstand the grueling campaign of the summer of 1781, which would leave the British army victorious, yet bottled up in their garrison at Charleston.

Readers will decide which view is correct.

CHAPTER 1

THE MAN FROM RHODE ISLAND: NATHANAEL GREENE

"Tis our business to study to avoid any considerable misfortune, and to take post where the Enemy will be obligd to fight us and not we them."—Nathanael Greene

THE GENERAL TURNED HIS HORSE and looked back along a narrow North Carolina dirt road. Heavy bands of trees and shrubs, with an occasional clearing, hugged much of its undulating route, which gradually sloped higher before breaking onto a small plateau about one-half mile to the northeast. The woods hid ravines, gullies, and several thin muddy ribbons of water. It was here he would make his stand.

An officer shouted a command and the marching men at the head of his column slowly responded. Pride swelled within the general as he watched his citizen-soldiers turn off the road and shuffle into one of the open areas. The place was about four hundred yards square, and the men took up a position near the southwest tree line behind a split-rail fence that ran perpendicular to their line of march. Two small cannons were wheeled into line and positioned near its center. Within a few minutes the flanks, stretching away into the thick timber and brush, would be hidden from view. Other men, more experienced veterans, would soon be forming on each end of the long line. A similar deployment was taking place several hundred yards behind them. The general's second line of battle waited in the forest's shadow and yet a third line was already in place another five hundred yards to the rear on the small plateau. He had selected each position even before his army reached the field.

Morale was good, much better than it should have been after weeks of frustrating marches through inclement weather on thin rations. The motley army was made up of about two-thirds militia, farmers mostly, their ranks leavened with a sprinkling of merchants and clerks. Most of them had decided only recently to risk their lives to defend their homes in support of the fledgling American nation. The balance of the army was comprised of hardened Regulars—veterans who had learned their trade the same way all hardened veterans have. Most of the men were glad the marching was at an end. They were ready to engage the enemy. They wanted to go home. The army was as ready as it would ever be, and it was larger than it had ever been. The terrain, perfect for defensive warfare, had been carefully chosen. The time for battle had arrived.

Satisfied with his dispositions, Nathanael Greene turned his horse and rode northeast for the third line, where a heavy line of veterans, studded with a pair of artillery pieces, had deployed on the L-shaped clearing on the crest. He knew he could count on his Continentals to stand and fight on the high ground, but how would his militia fare in the face of bayonet-wielding scarlet ranks? He would soon find out.

A musket shot away to the northeast was a tiny village of one hundred souls called Guilford Courthouse. It was March 14, 1781.

*   *   *

Nathanael Greene had arrived at Charlotte, North Carolina, three months earlier on December 2, 1780, the new commander for the Southern Department. Although

Nathanael Greene,

the task facing him must have seemed nearly insurmount-able, he had stared overwhelming odds in the face many times during his military career. Like his commanding general and mentor George Washington, Greene had learned how to turn adversity into advantage. But could he do so in the wilds of the Carolinas against the enemy's most experienced field commander? His predecessor had tried and failed miserably. Washington had lobbied Congress to install Greene to lead the effort, but that body had overruled him and instead appointed Horatio Gates in June 1780. It was not an unreasonable choice. Gates had, after all, defeated General John Burgoyne in upstate New York in the battles near Saratoga in 1777. Unfortunately for the Americans, he did not measure up to the challenge of warfare in the Carolina back country. On August 16, his mixed force of militia and Continentals had met Lord Charles Cornwallis's British army on the field at Camden, South Carolina. There, Gates presided over a spectacular defeat judged by most historians as the worse loss suffered by the Americans during the entire war.

By the time Greene arrived in Charlotte morale was at low ebb. The troops on hand numbered just 2,307, and most were untrained, ill-equipped, and without hope. Greene's task was straightforward enough: defeat Cornwallis and liberate the Carolinas. The devil, however, was in the details. Few would have wagered hard money that the former politician and private was up to the task.

The 38-year-old Greene was born in Potowomut (today's Warwick), Rhode Island, on August 7, 1742. His father was an iron founder, and Nathanael apprenticed under his watchful eye. The rigorous trade helped develop a strong body that soon stood nearly six feet in height. His eyes were a brilliant blue and accented a strong Roman nose that divided a long and somewhat pudgy face. Cobbled together with his high forehead and strong chin, these traits sketched a handsome and energetic young man. His family's roots were Quaker, and he was raised in that faith. Politics soon beckoned the younger Greene, who left the anvil behind for a seat in the state's General Assembly in 1770 at the age of twenty-eight. When war fervor gripped the colonies, he broke ranks with the pacific Quaker creed in the fall of 1774 and enthusiastically set about raising a company of militia. The decision seems to have come easy for him, though it brought about his prompt expulsion from the congregation. Given the future that awaited, it is more than ironic that his men refused to elect him captain. An injury suffered earlier in life had rendered the Rhode Islander partially lame, and a crippled head of a zealous militia company would not do. He did not complain of his plight. Instead, the wholly unpretentious Greene accepted their decision, took up a musket, and joined the ranks as a private.

Perhaps Greene realized he would not be long for the ranks. And indeed, he was not. The following May the maimed ex-Quaker was appointed brigadier general of militia, and a month later Congress elevated him to the rank of brigadier general in the Continental Army. This meteoric rise up the command ladder (the reasons for which remain hazy today) tossed him up on the doorstep of Virginian George Washington, the new commander of the Continental Army. The pair met for the first time in July 1775 in a camp outside Boston. Both the future president and the former blacksmith came away from the meeting thoroughly impressed, the former by Greene's calm self-assurance and keen intellect, and the latter with Washington's commanding presence and dignified manners. Washington was especially influenced by Greene's innate grasp of all things military—a characteristic he knew could never be taught. The neophyte soldier was also a good administrator and took care of his troops which, as Washington noted, "though raw, irregular, and undisciplined are under much better government than any around Boston." According to Alexander Hamilton, from that moment Washington "marked him as the object of his confidence . . . [and Greene] preserved it amidst all the checkered varities of military vicissitude." The two men would remain lifelong friends.

Greene repaid the Virginian's trust with dividends. During the siege of Boston he enjoyed a chair at Washington's frequent war councils, where his sage advice and grasp of logistics proved invaluable. After the British withdrew from Boston in March 1776, a new threat soon took shape when Sir William Howe, the Crown's commanding officer in North America, moved forward with a plan to invade and capture New York City. Although Washington tapped Greene to command the American forces on Long Island, he was absent when the British scored their smashing victory on the western side of the island at Brooklyn Heights that August. Sickness, perhaps malaria, had confined him and many more to their beds. A few days later Greene penned a note to his brother Jacob lamenting the fact that illness had kept him off the field. "Gracious God, to be confined at such a time!" he scribbled from his sickbed. Greene's lament is understandable, but his absence was in reality a stroke of temporary good fortune. His name was not stamped to a catastrophe whose outcome his presence could not have altered. The brush of defeat, which tarred others early with the taint of reverse, missed him entirely.

Washington, meanwhile, managed to slip his army across the East River to Manhattan, where a healthy Greene advised in a council of war that New York be abandoned and burned to the ground. "Not one benefit can arise to us from its preservation," he flatly told Washington. "A general and speedy retreat is absolutely necessary . . . I would burn the city and suburbs," he continued, for the city can never be recovered "without a superior naval force," something Green knew the colonists would likely never possess. Though harsh, his advice was militarily sound. But it was not followed, and the Americans endeavored to defend the city. Greene's militia was deployed on the southeast side of Manhattan Island in the vicinity of Kip's Bay. In the middle of September a flotilla of seventy-five flatboats, eleven bateaux, and two row-galleys, all jammed with redcoats, flooded across the East River and headed directly for his position. The crowded waterway reminded one poetically inclined observer of a larger-than-life clover field "in full bloom." Four divisions made the landing, including men under the command of a general named Charles Cornwallis. When the English navy added the weight of its iron to the threat confronting Greene's inexperienced Connecticut soldiers, his brigade turned tail to a man and fled. Greene, who was in his headquarters two miles north on Harlem Heights when the enemy crossed, once again missed the action. The next day would tell a different tale.

The Americans, including Greene's recently routed men, dug in across Harlem Heights, the narrow neck of land at the northwestern end of the island. When the head of the British army advanced against them on September 16, a spirited volley-trading skirmish ensued. Greene, together with other officers, rode up and down the line encouraging his men to stand firm and trade rounds with their counterparts. When the smoke drifted clear of the field they remained in possession of the heights. The two hours of sporadic fighting elated the Americans and punctured British pride. A jubilant Greene, who deemed it an "honor to command" his men in the action, proved that courage in the face of the enemy went hand-in-hand with his obvious intellectual prowess.

Still, he had much to learn and he promptly set out to prove it when he followed up the small tactical victory with a gross mistake of judgment compounded with a near-fatal error. The first dealt with his advice on the defense of Fort Washington. The earthen bastion covered a long stretch of high ground on the narrow tongue of land on the northernmost part of Manhattan Island between the Hudson and Harlem Rivers. Together with Fort Lee across the Hudson on the Jersey shore, it was intended to prevent the British from moving upriver. When an enemy warship penetrated the Hudson beyond the fort, General Washington advised abandoning the place. Greene sided with the fort's commander and disagreed, saying he did not believe "the Garrison to be in any great danger," and that they could be easily evacuated if the need arose. Though hindsight demonstrates how wrong he was, based upon the knowledge he possessed his arguments were generally sound. The British opened a massive attack against the fort on November 16 while Greene and Washington were visiting the place. They rowed quickly back to the Jersey side and watched the debacle from Fort Lee. The place fell quickly at a cost of some three thousand irreplaceable officers and men and tons of equipment, ammu nition, and supplies. Greene confided to his friend Henry Knox, "I feel made, vext, sick, and sorry." Greene still had much to learn but his education during the war's early years would echo loudly in 1781.

Five days later Sir Howe launched a surprise strike against Fort Lee with a column under his primary subordinate, Lord Charles Cornwallis. Only luck, something the Continental Army desperately needed more of, saved the garrison when one of Greene's aides, author Thomas Paine, spotted the move and Washington promptly ordered the place evacuated. As historian John Buchanan has aptly noted, "It was another lesson in the hard-earned education of Nathanael Greene. Luck, the handmaiden of every successful general, had been with him, however, and despite his blunder at Fort Washington his commander in chief did not lose faith in him." Washington's humiliated army retreated across New Jersey. Although Greene could not have known it, he and Cornwallis would meet again on other fields. The next several years of his "education" would take many forms.

Unable to catch up with and destroy Washington, Sir Howe decided to winter his troops. Fearing both a British attack and the arrival of the end of the year, when many in his army would leave for home with the expiration of their enlistments, Washington decided on a desperate gambit— he would attack first. His targets were Trenton and Princeton. He struck Howe's scattered forces just before the close of 1776. In the action Greene led one of the two major thrusts in a stunning victory over Howe's Hessians—the same men who had humiliated the Rhode Islander by capturing Fort Washington just six weeks earlier. At Princeton, Greene helped unite a fractured brigade and gained another well-earned victory. Morale soared. Washington's stock rose in nearly everyone's eyes. Congress adopted a resolution granting the general "full, ample and complete powers" to raise more troops and run the army essentially as he saw fit. His "military dictatorship," as one historian has wryly noted, was granted for a period of six months. But an American victory—if still a distant shot—suddenly seemed possible.

All wars are comprised of vast cesspools of petty politics, and Greene learned that lesson the hard way when he and other officers vigorously protested to Congress against the granting of a command rank major generalship to a French officer. If approved, the rank would have elevated him to a position of authority over many more experienced officers—like Nathanael Greene. Many men, including Greene, threatened to resign over the affair. The politicians resented what they considered to be meddling by the army officers but relented slightly and granted the Frenchman a staff appointment instead of a command rank. The move satisfied few, and Congress seethed over Greene's unyielding position. Because of this, years later the spiteful legislators would turn their backs on Greene when Washington petitioned them to name him as commander for the Southern Department.

More hard fighting followed in 1777 in the campaign for Philadelphia, the seat of the Colonial national government. The first battle was on September 11 at Brandywine Creek in Pennsylvania. General Howe, Washington's habitual nemesis, pinned the Americans in place and moved a large flanking force under Cornwallis and himself north and east against the right American flank. Poor intelligence led Washington to believe the move was a feint. When it became obvious he was wrong late that afternoon, Greene's two divisions were rushed north. In a trek one historian has compared to A. P. Hill's more famous forced march from Harpers Ferry to Sharpsburg during the Civil War, Greene drove his thousands of men four miles in a mere forty-five minutes. Demonstrating astonishing control, he immediately deployed them for battle as they arrived on the field, allowed the beaten Americans to retreat through his open ranks before conducting a gallant fighting withdrawal in the face of superior numbers. Three weeks later he waged another similar hot retreat at Germantown outside Philadelphia. The Colonial capital fell to the British, but the importance of keeping a tight control on one's marches and proper intelligence in the face of the enemy were not lost on Nathanael Greene.

After the army went into winter quarters in late 1777, a

committee of congressmen urged the Rhode Island native to leave his combat position and assume the reins of quartermaster general, a position Greene absolutely did not want. The glory of leading men in battle now coursed in his veins, and the proud officer—cognizant of the role he was playing in the unfolding history of the colonies—resisted the appointment. "No Body ever heard of a quarter Master in History," he wrote with contempt. When Washington learned of Greene's own pitiless foraging orders, opposition became all but impossible. He was just the man required to cleanse the country of supplies for the army. The pressure to accept proved overwhelming. Washington, he noted after accepting the job on March 2, 1778, "urged it upon me contrary to my wishes." To another he wrote, "I am taken out of the Line of splendor." A fellow officer received Greene's most heartfelt lament: "All of you will be immortalizing your selves in the golden pages of History, while I am confined to a series of drudgery to pave the way for it."

And it was a good thing he was so confined, for the American army might not have survived without him. Though he detested the job, Greene grasped immediately what needed to be done and did it, gathering and organizing supplies and improving the system of collection. His absence from the army, however, was keenly felt by Washington, who twice called upon him to lead troops in battle. Indeed, that arrangement may have been the price of Greene's acceptance of the quartermaster position. The first engagement during his dual tenure was at the confusing battle of Monmouth, New Jersey, on June 28, 1778. There, in charge of the right wing of Washington's revitalized army, Greene oversaw a defensive action that stood strong and tall in the face of a powerful advance of British Regulars led by the now familiar General Cornwallis. Though both sides claimed victory, the British withdrew from the field that night. There was little doubt that the Continental Army was coming of age. A second action on a smaller scale in Rhode Island later that summer saw similar results. Greene had risen through the ranks to become one of the Continental Army's finest combat officers.

From March of 1778 through July 1780, Greene labored to improve the army's logistical nightmare. His running feud with Congress flared up again and remained red hot through much of his tenure when that parsimonious body routinely refused to adequately fund his supply efforts. When Congress attempted to completely overhaul his department in the spring of 1780 he threw up his hands in disgust and resigned. Many in Congress were outraged and called for his head, but temporary personal salvation was found when Washington tapped him to command the Hudson Highlands. A more permanent form of deliverance arrived less then two weeks later hundreds of miles to the south when Horatio Gates lost his army at the battle of Camden, South Carolina, on August 16. The victor was an enemy Greene had met on several northern fields—Lord Charles Cornwallis. Thus far Congress had appointed three leaders to command the Southern Department; all three had proved abysmal failures. Who was capable of winning in the South? The legislators wrung their collective hands over the question for many weeks. Unable to bring themselves to select the right officer for the job but a man they despised, Congress turned the choice of a fourth commander over to Washington. The Virginian did not hesitate at all. On the fourteenth day of October 1780 he selected his favorite combat officer to pick up the shattered pieces of the south and carry the cause there to victory.

And so Nathanael Greene, the former iron founder, assemblyman, and private soldier—the man whose own recruits would not elect him company captain because of a bum leg—rode into Charlotte, North Carolina, on December 2, 1780. He knew the drill. He was familiar with what was expected of him.

There was no time to waste.

CHAPTER 2

THE CONSUMMATE PROFESSIONAL: CHARLES CORNWALLIS

"The damn rebels form well."—Lord Charles Cornwallis

ON THE AFTERNOON OF MARCH 14, 1781, information trickled in to a British army camp that the Americans had taken up a position just twelve miles to the north at a place called Guilford Courthouse. After weeks of avoiding contact was his counterpart really offering a pitched battle? Lord Charles Cornwallis was as aware as anyone that supplies and equipment were thin all the way around, especially so for his enemy. When the intelligence was confirmed that evening, the general wasted little time preparing his men for action. He would catch and destroy Nathanael Greene as soon as possible and bring this aggravating war in the southern colonies to a close.

About two thousand English and Hessian Regulars were up and on the move before sunrise the following morning. English cavalry under Banastre Tarleton had left hours earlier, fanning out into a miles-wide scarlet crescent to clear a path and scout ahead of the infantry column. If Cornwallis had anything to do with it, he would have his battle that very afternoon. He marched his veterans without breakfast.

The sun had not been up long when the sound of scattered firing in the distance reached the men marching in the van of Cornwallis's army. News arrived that the cavalry had encountered enemy horse, and a running skirmish had ensued. Before long other couriers bore word that a small body of American infantry had been located. Greene was indeed waiting for him.

Cornwallis must have smiled to himself. His opportunity to smash the amateur general and regain control of the Carolinas was at hand.

* * *

1st Marquess Cornwallis, 2nd Earl Cornwallis, Viscount Brome, Baron Cornwallis of Eye came into life in London, England, on December 31, 1738, the sixth child and eldest son. He was named Charles for his father. Unlike the man he would face at Guilford Courthouse forty-three years later, his line was descended from a family of high privilege and vested status.

Cornwallis spent two years at Eton College, Windsor, a prominent institution founded in 1440 by King Henry VI. He left in 1756 for a commission as ensign in the 1st Foot Grenadier Guards. The move seemed appropriate given his family's history and what was expected of the youth. Cornwallis could have followed the beaten path and learned his trade on the field, but instead chose to travel to Italy in the company of a Prussian tutor and attend the military academy at Turin. For reasons that remain obscure, he left the institution after only a few months.

Practical experience in the real world quickly followed. In 1758, two years after the outbreak of the Seven Years' War, Lord Brome (as Cornwallis was known at this time) served as a volunteer with England's allies, the Prussians. An appointment as aide-de-camp to the Marquis de Granby with the rank of captain came his way, and in that capacity he witnessed the August 1759 battle of Minden. This essential line staff experience was traded for a promotion to lieutenant colonel of the 12th Foot. In that capacity he acquired solid field tactical skills against the French in the 1761-62 battles at Vellinghausen, Wilhelmsthal, and Lutterberg. When word reached Cornwallis that his father had died suddenly in June 1762, the young officer returned home and assumed both the title 2nd Earl Cornwallis and his seat in the House of Lords.

Given the way history recalls him, it is ironic that Cornwallis's politics were very liberal, cut from the cloth of the "new Whigs" wing of Parliament led by William Pitt and William Petty, Earl of Shelburne. In other words, Cornwallis's sympathies rested wholly with the noisy colonists across the Atlantic, whose strident calls for reform appeared to be spiraling out of control. One of the most contentious debates in Parliament centered on the repeal of the Stamp Act in 1765, a law Cornwallis found distasteful and one he was strongly in favor of discarding. In fact, he was one of but five peers who voted in favor of its uncon-ditional repeal. Oddly, his outspoken criticisms of the king's policies endeared him to the monarch, and that same year he became his aide-de-camp. Exactly why George III enjoyed Cornwallis's company has never been satisfactori-ly explained. The following year Cornwallis boldly joined four other peers and cast his vote against the Declaratory Act, a noxious bit of legislation declaring that England had the right to pass any laws regarding the colonies it saw fit. That same year Cornwallis bought the colonelcy of the 33rd Foot.

Two years later this rising star of English politics found the love of his life. Jemima Tullekin Jones was the daughter of an infantry officer, and thus not of the same familial stature as his own, but she was a lovely woman and the young earl married her. She bore him two children, a boy and a girl. By all accounts it was a happy union, though destined to end prematurely.

When war finally broke out between the colonies and Britain, there was never any doubt where Cornwallis's loy-alties rested. When the young earl volunteered for service he was appointed major general in late 1775 and shipped

Lord Charles Cornwallis.

off to North America early the next year. He sailed from Cork, Ireland, with seven regiments and, after a difficult voyage, rendezvoused with Sir Henry Clinton off the Carolinas. Clinton's orders were to "restore the authority of the King's government in the four southern provinces." In reality that meant taking the important port of Charleston, South Carolina, the natural launching point for any large-scale campaign in the south. The mid-summer attempt, led by Clinton and naval officer Sir Peter Parker, has come down through history as the battle of Sullivan's Island. It was more spectacular debacle than battle. It was also wholly uninfluenced by Cornwallis's presence. Like Nathanael Greene's first combat in the colonies, Cornwallis too avoided having his name associated with a conspicuous failure. Brighter fields of battle in the middle colonies awaited his arrival.

Abandoning the hapless effort against Charleston, Clinton and Cornwallis sailed north for New York City, where a massive British effort was underway by Sir William Howe to defeat George Washington's army and wrest away control of the city from the colonists. On August 22, Howe unleashed his primary effort against western Long Island. Of the fifteen thousand troops landed that day a sizeable reserve force was under Cornwallis's command. The battle was the first time the Americans and British met in the open field. The outcome was exactly as the latter expected it would be.

Sir Howe's next move was carefully planned but long in coming. Cornwallis was placed in charge of a mammoth amphibious operation against Manhattan at Kip's Bay on September 15. Once General Washington was pushed north of Harlem Heights, the British set their eyes on a pair of forts guarding entry to the upper Hudson River—Fort Lee, on the New Jersey side, and Fort Washington, on northern Manhattan Island. Fort Washington fell to a fast and overwhelming Hessian attack on November 16 and on November 19, Cornwallis landed with forty-five hundred men about five miles above Fort Lee. Once again he was at the head of an amphibious operation, and once again he pulled it off without a hitch.

Washington withdrew south across New Jersey, and Sir Howe closed out the Campaign of 1776 by ordering his troops into winter quarters. Showing a disdain for his enemy, Howe established a string of outposts running from Staten Island southwest to Princeton, a weak line without depth that meandered eighty miles across the Jersey countryside. For Cornwallis, the winter brought a chance to go home to England, where he longed to see his wife Jemima and their two children. Washington, however, had other plans.

On December 26, 1776, Washington and his army crossed the Delaware River in a multipronged advance, marched on Trenton, and fought a brisk but short engagement that ended with the surrender of almost one thousand veteran Hessians, with another one hundred and twenty killed and wounded. American losses totaled but four wounded. Among other things Howe canceled Cornwallis's leave. The earl was about to board ship in New York for England when Howe's orders reached him: return at once and take command in southern New Jersey.

Angered by the canceled leave and burning with ambition to rise in command, Cornwallis set out to crush Washington. On January 2, 1777, he deployed several regiments totaling some twelve hundred men as a rear guard at Princeton and a similar number at Maidenhead before striking out for Trenton at the head of fifty-five hundred men and twenty-eight artillery pieces. The advance was disputed almost every step of the way by the plucky Americans. By the time the van reached the outskirts of Trenton, the Americans were conducting a fighting withdrawal worthy of Europe's finest veterans. Late that afternoon Cornwallis found Washington's men deployed below Trenton on a ridge behind the far side of Assunpink Creek. One of his generals urged an immediate attack in the failing light of day. The usually energetic and prompt Cornwallis demurred. The Delaware River blocked much of Washington's route of retreat. The American had marched himself into a box and would be ripe for picking in the morning. It was a decision that would haunt Cornwallis for the rest of his days.

The temperature dropped that night, freezing the muddy roads solid. Washington used the hardened roads to march the bulk of his forces the dozen or so miles to Princeton around the stationary British left flank where three enemy regiments waited, blissfully unaware of his approach. Cornwallis awoke the following morning to both gunfire in his left rear and one of the greatest shocks of his professional life: the upstart Virginian with the ragtag army had stolen a march on the professional soldier and inflicted a sharp defeat on one of his own detachments. Showing the

Sir William Howe.

energy by which he is rightly known, Cornwallis drove his men to Princeton with incredible speed, where he narrowly missed engaging Washington's rear guard. Although he followed his enemy closely, Washington made an unexpected turn and Cornwallis lost him. One can only imagine the language Cornwallis used to address himself that day. As one Revolutionary War historian so aptly observed, "So ended the New Jersey Campaign of 1776, which had ignored the calendar and lapped over a few days into 1777."

Cornwallis's mental wound festered during the inaction of the next several months until the arrival of spring and a new campaign that brought with it fresh opportunities for him to burnish his tarnished reputation. To the bafflement of Washington, Howe withdrew his forces to Staten Island. By June 30 the British had evacuated New Jersey.

Sir Howe, whose brother Admiral Lord Howe commanded the British fleet, had been quietly massing ships for two months in New York harbor. On July 8 he loaded his men, horses, and equipment aboard, and then waited.

After two weeks of temporizing Howe set sail on July 23—and vanished. Without a navy Washington had no way of knowing where Howe was heading. Several anxious weeks passed until word finally arrived that the fleet was in the northeast Chesapeake opposite the head of the Elk River. Washington reacted immediately by issuing orders for the separated pieces of his army to assemble around Philadelphia.

Howe began disembarking his men on August 25, but his army remained stationary for several days. He was not a man to be rushed. The men rested and stretched, regaining their land legs for the trials ahead. Howe's army of some 12,500 effectives was organized into two grand divisions, seventy-five hundred men under Lord Cornwallis and five thousand under Hessian General Wilhelm von Knyphausen. On August 28 the inland phase of the campaign for Philadelphia got underway with a move to Elkton. Five more quiet days passed. Brief but unimportant skirmishes flared hither and yon while the opponents sized up one another for the pitched battle that was now all but inevitable.

Knyphausen's division was the first to move on September 2. Cornwallis's division, accompanied by Sir Howe, left the next morning by a different route. By September 8 Howe's army was united and driving north and east. Washington moved to intercept him, taking up a position the following day along the Brandywine Creek, his center opposite Chadd's Ford. Howe planned to pin Washington in place at Chadd's Ford with a diversion by Knyphausen's division while Cornwallis moved his men north and east to turn their right flank.

On the morning of September 11, 1777, both British divisions were on the move early. Knyphausen's marched about 5:00 A.M., heading east toward Washington's center. Cornwallis and Howe, meanwhile, had marched out an hour earlier than Knyphausen, heading north to Osbourne Hill more than one mile east of the Brandywine, two miles from the nearest enemy pickets—and squarely in the right-rear of Washington's army. They arrived at 2:30 P.M. Cornwallis had marched his men almost seventeen miles in less than eleven hours. Few could have accomplished it as smoothly as he had.

Initially, Washington had suspected the move against Chadd's Ford represented Howe's main attack, but when the British did not attempt to force a crossing he began suspecting a ruse. Before noon reports trickled in that a large body of the enemy was moving around his northern flank. Conflicting information worked to Cornwallis's advantage and kept Washington guessing as to Howe's true course of action. Finally, uncontrovertible evidence arrived when a cavalry officer reported two British brigades in the vicinity of Osborne Hill. Washington ordered his right wing under the command of General John Sullivan to shift north to oppose the thrust while he remained at Chadd's Ford with Nathanael Greene's division and two other brigades—just in case. Sullivan marched with celerity and formed his men on a round hill near the Birmingham Meetinghouse on good defensive ground, though slightly ahead of the two brigades that were already there protecting the American right flank. The deployment impressed the unflappable Cornwallis, who noted to an aide, "The damn rebels form well."

Cornwallis ordered his divisions forward a bit after 4:00 P.M. The right side of Sullivan's line opened on the Hessians opposite them. For Knyphausen, Cornwallis's battle was his signal to open a second front against the American center to pin them in place and keep reinforcements from moving north. For a time he was successful and the fighting there ebbed and flowed with some regularity.

For Cornwallis, the initial fighting could not have gone better. Within a few minutes the right side of Sullivan's line was reeling in retreat. A few minutes more and the far left of the line cracked and melted away, fighting as they fled, but fleeing nonetheless. The center, however, stood firm and traded volleys and artillery fire at close range. According to one survivor, "Cannon balls flew thick and many, and small arms roared like the rolling of a drum." Showing a keen appreciation for the field's key objective, Cornwallis pressed the enemy while shifting his men east toward Dilworth in an effort to flank the Americans and cut the road leading to Philadelphia. After almost two hours of continuous fighting the remaining American stalwarts began to fall out of line. A retreat was ordered. Within a few minutes the withdrawal had devolved into a near rout. The critical moment of the battle had arrived.

Elated with the performance of his men, Cornwallis displayed the killer instinct by ordering an immediate and vigorous pursuit. Unfortunately for the British, at that very moment American reinforcements arrived on the field in the form of a division dispatched by Washington from Chadd's Ford. Without delay Nathanael Greene ordered his trotting column into a line of battle while simultaneously opening his ranks so his fleeing comrades could slip through to safety and re-form in the rear. There were now two superb tacticians on the field.

Cornwallis was unruffled by the appearance of fresh enemy troops. His infantry continued to step forward and fire, trading volleys that slowly but surely drove Greene's men rearward. The Americans re-formed in a good defensive position along the road from Dilworth, about one mile from the original action. There, heavy fighting and numerous bayonet charges were absorbed and repelled. Cornwallis assaulted for almost another hour, but was unable to break through before the sun went down. Greene ordered his men to form up and fall back, and Cornwallis—mindful of the exhausted state of his men and the difficult terrain, made no attempt at pursuit. The bulk of Washington's broken army flooded east toward Chester. Except for Greene's redoubtable division, there was not a single organized body of American troops worthy of the name. Cornwallis, meanwhile, linked up with Knyphausen on the east side of the stream. The battle of Brandywine was now a part of history.

A few more days of maneuvering and Philadelphia was ready to fall. On September 26, Howe offered Lord Cornwallis the honor of taking possession of the Colonial capital. He entered the city at 11:00 A.M. at the head of his column, dressed in a resplendent scarlet coat adorned with golden lace. For Cornwallis, the heady balm of victory went a long way toward soothing the anguish he had suffered from the Princeton debacle nine months earlier.

When the 1777 campaign approached its end, Cornwallis took leave and arrived in England in January 1778. Major changes rode the seas with him. Sir William Howe, who had long disagreed with King George III's handling of the Colonial rebellion, submitted his resignation. Cornwallis fancied himself ready to fill Howe's shoes and ached for the position, but London had a long memory. The embarrassment of Cornwallis's sleepy performance at Trenton, where Washington and his army slipped out of his grasp, persisted. Lord Jeffrey Amherst was offered the command. Amherst, a keen observer of the war and Howe's travails there, judiciously declined the honor. The simple process of elimination forced the king's hand. Howe's resignation was reluctantly accepted and a lesser officer, Sir Henry Clinton, was elevated to the supreme command. In June 1778, the rejected and embittered Cornwallis returned to America as Clinton's executive officer. Unlike Howe's, Charles Cornwallis's attempt to resign was bruskly refused.

Cornwallis's return was none too soon, for a significant shift in strategy was at hand. Howe's dearly bought capture of Philadelphia had turned out to be no prize at all. The rebels had simply moved their seat of government and the expensive occupation divided and dissipated the understrength British effort. Sir Clinton's orders were to evacuate the city. Within days of his arrival Cornwallis was marching with Clinton's army of thirteen thousand men for New York. Washington's revitalized and slightly larger force was met near Monmouth Courthouse. Clinton ordered an immediate attack against the American left flank. In weather that topped one hundred degrees the men moved forward with great elan, but a steady fire well delivered beat them back. Piqued at the failure, Clinton ordered Cornwallis to attack Washington's right flank, held by his Brandywine nemesis Nathanael Greene. Cornwallis advanced with his infantry and personally led the attack into a withering blaze of musketry supported by a deadly crossfire of artillery. An artillery duel closed the contest and darkness drew a curtain over the fighting. Both armies claimed the field, but Clinton withdrew during the night. The rebels had stood toe-to-toe with the British. Although no one knew it, the last major battle in the northern colonies was over.

A week later Cornwallis was in New York, and a few months later he was again on a ship bound for England, this time with orders from Clinton to press the government for reinforcements. His arrival was greeted with depressing news: his beloved Jemima was seriously ill. Unable to bear being away from her when she most needed him, he resigned from his position in North America. Jemima lingered for many weeks before dying in February 1779. Cornwallis was beyond consoling. Her death, he told his brother-in-law, "effectually destroyed all my hopes of happiness in this world." Three months passed before Cornwallis was able to pick himself up and rejoin the living. America beckoned. The professional soldier offered his services to his king, who gladly accepted them. "I am now returning to America," wrote the widower to his brother, "not with views of conquest and ambition, nothing brilliant can be expected in that quarter; but I found this country quite unsupportable to me. I must shift the scene; I have many friends in the American army [British army fighting in America]; I love that army, and flatter myself that I am not quite indifferent to them."

Sir Clinton had dispatched Cornwallis to England to

bring back reinforcements. When he arrived in New York in July 1779 empty-handed, an angry Clinton scribbled out a resignation letter. If the king would not support his effort, he would no longer fight for him. Although it would take months to get a reply, Clinton was confident it would be accepted and that Cornwallis would take his place. Although he pretended otherwise, the ambitious and driven second officer recognized and welcomed the opportunity to advance his career to a level that seemed permanently closed to him just a few months earlier. The dispatch of the resignation letter, however, triggered subtle changes in the pair's relationship and brought forth animosities that had been but shallowly buried for almost two years.

With the 1779 campaign season over in the north, Clinton turned his eyes southward toward the Carolinas and Georgia. His own army was large, about twenty-five thousand strong, and the time seemed right to subjugate the south once and for all with a campaign beginning in South Carolina and driving northward through North Carolina and into Virginia. Clinton hoped to stimulate the Loyalists in large numbers while the Carolinians were disheartened by a recent defeat at Savannah and the disappearance of the French navy. Leaving behind Knyphausen and a large army to watch General Washington, Clinton left New York in late December 1779 with eighty-five hundred well-equipped men. Cornwallis was his second in command. Trouble sailed with them.

The command situation was awkward in the extreme and boded ill for British arms. Commander-in-chief Clinton was still awaiting word on his resignation submitted months earlier to England, while his ambitious subordinate and likely replacement—who would inherit whatever strategic situation Clinton left for him—worked at his elbow. Though he looked on him with reasonable suspicion, Sir Clinton involved Cornwallis in every discussion of strategy and relied on his advice. Together the pair did the best they could to bring Charleston under successful siege by isolating it on its land approaches. And then it arrived. The dispatch from London both men had long awaited reached them on March 19, 1780; the king, Lord George Germain advised Clinton, "was too well satisfied with your conduct to wish to see the command of his forces in any other hands." As might be expected, the news crushed both men. Clinton remained on the hook, and Cornwallis's dream of high command was not to be.

It did not take Cornwallis long to reveal a side of his personality he usually kept hidden from view: pettiness. Since he would not be taking command after all, he informed his shocked commander, he no longer wanted to be consulted on matters of strategy. Why be held responsible for faulty decisions with no chance of reaping a reward? The news must have dropped Sir Clinton's mouth open. Instead of ordering his presence at war councils, Clinton unlocked a box long closed and denounced Cornwallis for leaking news of his resignation and turning other officers against him. There is no evidence to support the accusation. Cornwallis, meanwhile, hurled accusations of his own, all of a trivial nature. The relationship, so long strained, was now beyond repair.

With neither man able to work with the other, Cornwallis asked for a separate command. He was given Lieutenant Colonel James Webster's corps outside Charleston along the Cooper River. The arrangement worked as well as could have been expected, the siege moved relentlessly forward, and on May 12, 1780, Charleston surrendered. More than five thousand men and tons of supplies were lost to the American cause. An elated Clinton, who set sail for New York on June 5, left behind him the job of reducing and subjugating the rest of the Carolinas, a difficult task he gladly passed along to Cornwallis.

Garrisons at Charleston, Georgetown (in the Low Country sixty miles northeast of Charleston), Beaufort, and Savannah were maintained to protect the coastline. Because the only way to conquer the back country was to occupy it, Cornwallis set about establishing a string of interior garrisons. The South Carolina real estate grab began on May 18 when Cornwallis left Charleston to occupy Camden, South Carolina, a small but bustling place 115 miles to the northwest. It was easily seized and initially garrisoned with twenty-five hundred Regulars and Tories. In order to secure the country between Camden and Georgetown, two battalions of Highlanders moved north and east of Camden to Cheraw, on the Big Pee Dee River just a handful of miles below the North Carolina border. Three more battalions tramped eighty-five miles west of Camden to an important trading post called Ninety-Six. From there, the line of outposts stretched fifty miles due south to the Savannah River and Augusta, Georgia, which was occupied with another detachment of Tories. Clinton was gone, Lord Cornwallis had his independent command. What he would do with it remained to be seen.

Government officials in London were completely mistaken about the true state of affairs facing His Majesty's forces in the Carolinas. Many members of Parliament believed the entire south was brimming with loyal men waiting to turn out for the king. Lord Cornwallis's appreciation of reality was almost as wide of the mark. After his thrusts had dispersed tepid opposition, he wrote Clinton at the end of June that the "end to all resistance in South Carolina" had been effectively achieved. If the French did not intervene in strength, he continued, "I can leave South Carolina in security and march the beginning of September into the back part of North Carolina, with the greatest probability of reducing that province to its duty." Years of fighting against a determined foe who had thus far refused to break should have served notice in ample portions that resistance was nowhere close to being at an end. Cornwallis's complete miscalculation of the situation is baffling.

Cornwallis quickly discovered how wrong he was when he learned on August 9 that the hero of Saratoga, General Horatio Gates, had been appointed to take command of the

General Horatio Gates.

Continental army in South Carolina. Gates, whom Cornwallis had never met in battle, was marching south toward the seven-hundred-man garrison at Camden under the command of Lord Francis Rawdon. The British could ill afford to lose the important crossroads town, and Cornwallis knew it. He ordered reinforcements to assemble at Camden and left Charleston on horseback, arriving on the evening of August 13. Although it numbered only 2,239 men, the British army at Camden brimmed with Regulars and hardened volunteers. Gates was rumored to have double that number. The confident Cornwallis, however, had faith in both his generalship and the superior fighting quality of his men. They could best any army Gates could field. Equivocation was not a substantial feature of Cornwallis's nature.

Ironically, on August 15 both generals implemented a similar plan: a night march to get into position for a possible attack the next day. At about 2:00 A.M. the following morning, advance cavalry elements of the opposing forces stumbled into one another on the old Waxhaws Road several miles north of Camden above Saunder's Creek. Both sides pulled back and prepared for battle as soon as it was light enough to fight.

The terrain upon which the armies found themselves formed a constricted field of battle less than one mile wide, divided by the Waxhaws Road and bounded on both sides by swampy terrain. Flanking operations were out of the question. The day promised to be an affair of volleys and bayonets, and that suited Cornwallis just fine. He formed his men before dawn in accordance with standard European tradition, his finest troops holding the position of honor on the right of the line. With the road as his guide he divided his army into two wings. James Webster's Regulars marched to the right and took their place there. They included the 23rd and 33rd Foot and five companies of Scottish Highlanders aligned behind them in reserve. The left wing, under the command of Lord Rawdon, was comprised of experienced Tories, Irish volunteers, a Royal North Carolina regiment and militia. In reserve was Banastre Tarleton's veteran legion of horse and foot. Four pieces of artillery were unlimbered in the center of his line. Cornwallis's conviction of victory was plainly evident: he formed for action with Saunder's Creek behind him. The first light of day revealed that Gates had deployed his army in essentially the same fashion, with his best troops on his right flank. Cornwallis could not have been more pleased with the arrangement. His finest Regulars were standing face to face with Gates's untried and untrained militia.

To this day it is impossible to know what was coursing through Gates's mind when he aligned his troops as he did. Certainly he recalled nothing of his twenty-four years of service in the British army. His right front was composed of about nine hundred veteran Maryland and Delaware infantry under the command of General Jean, Baron de Kalb, one of the Continental Army's finest subordinate commanders. Three of the small Maryland regiments straddled the road in reserve, two hundred yards behind the front line. Gates joined them there with his staff. The left front was constructed entirely of militia from North Carolina and Virginia, about twenty-five hundred untried and inexperienced soldiers. A few score cavalry and other light infantry were behind them. Seven pieces of artillery dotted the line. The exact strength of Gates's army is open to some question, but the best estimates place it at thirty-seven hundred men. There was not a hint of a breeze, a minor trick nature played that day that would ill-serve the luckless Gates.

Cornwallis opened the battle early by doing exactly what he should have done: attack with his Regulars directly into Gates's waiting militia. Webster's wing slowly tramped forward in perfect columns, deployed into line of battle, and moved forward without interruption. Cornwallis, as he always did and in stark contrast to Gates, stationed himself close behind the front lines. Webster's men advanced "with great vigour [and] in good order and with the cool intrepidity of experienced British soldiers," he wrote in his report of the battle. As Webster's eight hundred veterans marched forward they watched as Gates's twenty-five hundred waiting militia fumbled about for their bayonets and tried to lock them in place on the ends of their muskets—something the green soldiers had never done in the face of a professional enemy. They would never use them. The redcoats quickened their pace and yelled in unison and the Virginians and North Carolinians began melting away, first as individuals, then in clusters, and finally in a wave their officers were unable to halt. Panic, wrote one of them after the battle, is like electricity. "It operates simultaneously—like sympathy, it is irresistible when it touches." Sweaty American hands dropped hundreds of loaded muskets in the frantic effort to avoid being speared by English steel. One militia regiment from North Carolina, positioned near the road next to the Delaware Regulars, stood its ground and traded several volleys with the approaching enemy. Otherwise, the entire left wing of Gates's army was gone.

The fight on the other side of the field, at least initially, went well for the Americans. Rawdon's infantry had advanced shortly after Webster's, but General de Kalb's stalwarts were not about to drop their muskets and run. Instead, the men from Maryland and Delaware stood tall and twice repulsed Rawdon's infantry. De Kalb, who was wounded early and often at Camden, launched an attack of his own. The thrust reached close quarters and nearly broke through Rawdon's wavering volunteers. Cornwallis rode directly into the thick of the action and inspired his men to stand their ground. He sat his horse in the thick of the fray "with great coolness, in the midst of a heavier fire than the oldest soldier remembers" wrote one of Rawdon's inspired Irish captains.

While de Kalb and Rawdon were slugging it out at close range, Webster demonstrated once again his outstanding tactical abilities and why Cornwallis had such faith in him. Webster reined in his victorious Regulars east of the road, wheeled them to the left, and advanced in an effort to roll up General de Kalb's flank and rear. The old soldier and his veterans, however, had no idea what was coming and so could do little to prepare for it when it arrived. Although some of them must have seen knots of the militia running for the rear, few of them appreciated the magnitude of the disaster unfolding only a few hundred yards away on the far side of Waxhaws Road. The gun smoke there hung motionless in the day's dead calm, obscuring almost everything from view.

A few moments later the first glimpse of approaching death was spotted tramping out of the gray shroud of smoke. The Maryland infantrymen held in reserve were hastily ordered forward by the wounded de Kalb while the remaining North Carolina militia wheeled to greet Webster's Regulars. Somehow these men dug deep enough to bravely stand their ground and grind Webster's attack to a bloody standstill.

About one hour had elapsed since Webster's men had stepped off to the attack. The climax of the battle had arrived and Cornwallis knew it. With the touch of a battle-field master—as he was on this day at Camden—Cornwallis ordered Banastre Tarleton's cavalry to swing around and attack the American rear. The battle now began to resemble, though on a much smaller scale, the great Carthaginian victory over the Romans at Cannae, with Tarleton's horsemen reprising the role of Hasdrubal's Spanish cavalry. Acting with the celerity for which he had become famous, Tarleton sliced around the American left and into their rear, sealing off their last avenue of escape. With Tarleton's troopers slashing and hacking, Rawdon's volunteers standing firm in front, and Webster's veterans pressing from the flank, armed opposition ended quickly. A handful of Continentals slipped to safety through the swampy ground to the west. The battle had lasted but one hour. Cornwallis gave Tarleton free reign to pursue the fleeing Americans and he did so over twenty miles of equipment-strewn ground before finally turning back. When Cornwallis learned that the Prussian soldier Baron de Kalb had fallen, he spurred his horse to where the officer lay. He was found on a litter, punctured by eleven bayonet, sword, and ball wounds. "I am sorry, sir, to see you, not sorry that you are vanquished, but sorry to see you so badly wounded," offered Cornwallis. De Kalb's response, if he made one, is lost to history. Cornwallis ordered that he be removed to Camden and given medical treatment. The gallant Prussian died three days later.

The loss at Camden staggered the American cause and threw the Colonialists into a deep gloom. Gates, who had fled before the fighting ended, left behind him a shattered army that all but ceased to exist. Although losses seem never to have been formally presented, approximately two hundred and fifty were killed and eight hundred wounded. Because the British held the field, every wounded American was captured. Cornwallis reported his casualties as sixty-eight killed and two hundred and fifty-six wounded, or about 14 percent of his effective force. It was a reasonable price to pay for such a crushing victory.

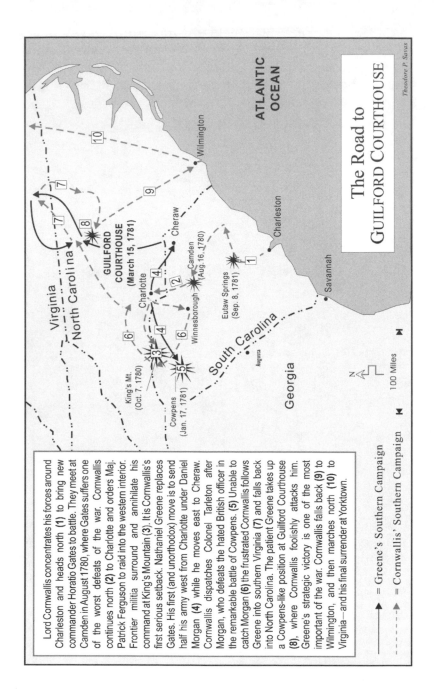

The Road to
GUILFORD COURTHOUSE

Theodore P. Savas

ATLANTIC OCEAN

Virginia
North Carolina
South Carolina
Georgia

Wilmington
Charleston
Savannah
Augusta

GUILFORD COURTHOUSE
(March 15, 1781)
Cheraw
Camden
(Aug. 16, 1780)
Charlotte
Winnesborough
Eutaw Springs
(Sep. 8, 1781)
King's Mt.
(Oct. 7, 1780)
Cowpens
(Jan. 17, 1781)

N
100 Miles

Lord Cornwallis concentrates his forces around Charleston and heads north **(1)** to bring new commander Horatio Gates to battle. They meet at Camden in August 1780, where Gates suffers one of the worst defeats of the war. Cornwallis continues north **(2)** to Charlotte and orders Maj. Patrick Ferguson to raid into the western interior. Frontier militia surround and annihilate his command at King's Mountain **(3)**. It is Cornwallis's first serious setback. Nathaniel Greene replaces Gates. His first (and unorthodox) move is to send half his army west from Charlotte under Daniel Morgan **(4)** while he moves east to Cheraw. Cornwallis dispatches Colonel Tarleton after Morgan, who defeats the hated British officer in the remarkable battle of Cowpens. **(5)** Unable to catch Morgan **(6)** the frustrated Cornwallis follows Greene into southern Virginia **(7)** and falls back into North Carolina. The patient Greene takes up a Cowpens-like position at Guilford Courthouse **(8)**, where Cornwallis foolishly attacks him. Greene's strategic victory is one of the most important of the war. Cornwallis falls back **(9)** to Wilmington, and then marches north **(10)** to Virginia—and his final surrender at Yorktown.

→ = Greene's Southern Campaign

---→ = Cornwallis' Southern Campaign

CHAPTER 3

PRELUDE TO GUILFORD COURTHOUSE

"I am not altogether without hopes of prescribing some bounds to the ravages of the enemy."—Nathanael Greene

BOTH SIR HENRY CLINTON AND LORD CHARLES CORNWALLIS basked in the aftermath of the Camden fight. They loathed one another, but they also carried a mutual grievance against the Crown for slights more perceived than actual. King George III, it will be recalled, had been reluctant to replace Howe with Clinton—and had then refused to accept the latter's resignation if only to prevent the elevation of Cornwallis to a position few in London believed him capable of holding. The smashing success at Camden offered Clinton and Cornwallis vindication for their individual military abilities. The decision to leave Cornwallis with an independent command in the south with orders to drive inland proved Clinton's strategic ability (so he believed, anyway), and Cornwallis finally had the first independent battlefield victory of his career. The only question now was how to capitalize on such a victory.

Clinton's foggy idea of a march toward victory included the gradual squeezing of Virginia by occupying Delaware and subjugating North Carolina. The latter move, suggested Clinton, was something Cornwallis was now in a position to attempt. Camden had crowned him as the all but undisputed master of South Carolina and Georgia. As long as the king's hold on those colonies was not jeopardized, cautioned Clinton, the conquest of North Carolina was an acceptable undertaking. The pugnacious Cornwallis was all for offensive warfare. After all, a belligerent North Carolina posed a threat to his current position, but its vanquishment would allow him to march north on roads leading to Virginia, Pennsylvania, and glory. If the Americans were forced out of North Carolina, he postulated, the entire South would "fall without much resistance and be retained without much difficulty."

Using Camden as a magnet, Cornwallis pulled in reinforcements from different points of the compass, gathered supplies and wagons, and prepared to launch his new campaign. With his twenty-two hundred men organized into two large divisions, he marched north on September 8 to the Waxhaws. The last week of the month found him again on the move and again moving north, this time with his eyes set forty miles away on Charlotte, North Carolina. The van of the army approached the small town from the southeast. In 1780, the place consisted of but twenty houses and two main streets. As the British approached the courthouse along East Trade Street, scattered shots rang out; the head of the column had run directly into a small but stubborn blocking force of militia. The meeting triggered an interesting and instructive skirmish.

Given their small numbers, the defenders of Charlotte were an aggressive lot. They totaled but one hundred and fifty militia, eighty of whom were mounted, and all of whom were under the command of William Richardson Davie, a capable partisan officer determined to show Cornwallis that North Carolina would not fall as easily under his despotic heel as had her sister colony to the south. Davie had carefully and cleverly deployed his men for the coming fight. In the center, twenty dismounted dragoons were positioned behind a chest-high stone wall fronting on open ground recessed into the town and in front of the courthouse. The rest of his men were stationed well in advance on either side of the wall, hidden away in houses, yards, and gardens. With Banastre Tarleton nursing a fever, the Legion's horsemen were led by Major George Hanger. He displayed the same reckless disdain for the enemy possessed by his superior, though without Tarleton's commensurate tactical ability. When he spotted Davie's dismounted dragoons, Hanger immediately launched his cavalry against them. Davie and his men coolly stood their ground and loosed a volley at sixty yards. Horses and riders tumbled to the ground. Hanger's cavalry fell back amid another hail of musket balls and re-formed while General James Webster's light infantry moved forward on either side to engage Davie's advanced flanks. Embarrassed by the repulse, Hanger launched a second direct attack. This, too, was thrown back with loss.

Cornwallis was hardly pleased by the situation waiting for him when he reached the front. His superb cavalry were milling about in confusion, worried that they had ridden into an ambush, and his entire army was being held up by a handful of North Carolina militia. His usual aplomb receded and his anger rose to the fore. How could militia stop his soldiers? Had his men learned nothing from their experiences in the colonies? "Charge them!" he shouted. Not a horse advanced. Incredulous, the general yelled that they had "everything to lose" by refusing to advance, "but nothing to gain!" One onlooker believed he was referring to the Legion's vaunted reputation, which seemed about to be tarnished.

Webster's infantry saved Lord Cornwallis from further embarrassment. The general hotly repeated the attack order to both infantry and cavalry. Apparently Hanger's horse did not move forward a third time, although reports on this score are contradictory. Webster's Regulars, however, heeded their orders as they always did. They smartly pressed in Davie's flanks and the partisan leader wisely evacuated the field. Webster's pursuit, perhaps in company with a handful of cavalrymen, may have killed and wounded up to one-fifth of the militia force, though Davie claimed but five dead and six wounded. Cornwallis reported his losses as fifteen killed and wounded. The road into North Carolina was again open.

The Charlotte skirmish embarrassed and enraged Cornwallis, who was not used to seeing his Regulars cower in the face of American militia. His solution to the roadblock—attack, and attack immediately—revealed again his bull-headed aggressive attitude. As he had witnessed on several fields in the north, and now Camden and Charlotte in the south, American militia were unable to stand in the face of a determined attack. As far as Cornwallis was concerned, the lesson was clear: when confronted by militia, advance aggressively and seize the field at the point of the bayonet. It was a reasonable response and one that had thus far served him well. It was also a predictable response that a more capable and shrewd opponent might use to advantage.

But now unbeknownst to Cornwallis, the campaign was about to spin out of control because of a decision he had made three months earlier that was about to come back and haunt him.

*   *   *

Earlier that summer in June, Cornwallis had dispatched Major Patrick Ferguson, a thirty-six-year-old native of Scotland, together with several hundred Tory militia, westward into the back country of South Carolina to protect his far left flank. Ferguson did an outstanding job and while camped along the Little River augmented his numbers to some four thousand men. Carolina Loyalists all, they flocked to his banner with promises of warfare against the rebels and revenge against their neighbors. He organized them into seven regiments. Two days after Cornwallis's column stumbled into Davie's men in Charlotte, Ferguson paroled a captured rebel at Gilbert Town, North Carolina, telling him to spread the word in the mountains that if the rebels "did not desist from their opposition to British arms and take protection under his standard, he would march his army over the mountains, hang their leaders, and lay their country waste with fire and sword."

The Overmountain men, as they were known then and are called today, hailed primarily from the region that would one day be eastern Tennessee. Ferguson's pompous nonsense did not sit well with them. Someone organized a call to arms, and hundreds of men gathered at Sycamore Shoals. The pursuit of Ferguson was underway. A short time later the men elected Colonel William Campbell to act as their overall commander. Reinforcements steadily trickled in, and on October 6, 1780, a scout arrived with news that Ferguson and part of his force were camped just twenty-eight miles north on King's Mountain, a rock- and tree-studded hill crowned with an open summit just below the North Carolina border and forty miles west of Charlotte. Campbell and nine hundred mounted men headed out for a long overnight ride bound on revenge.

The next afternoon, October 7, Campbell and his small army of mountain men decided to surround the hill and attack it from four sides. They slipped into their respective positions and began working their way toward the summit, where Ferguson and his eleven hundred Tories waited blissfully unaware of what was to befall them. The fight opened about 3:00 P.M. when two of Campbell's columns traded fire with the Tories while the other two attack groups closed in for the kill. Ferguson, who was smart enough to realize his dire predicament, had already dispatched a rider to Cornwallis seeking a relief column. Now he had to hold out until help arrived. His situation, however, steadily deteriorated. He resorted to bayonet attacks in an attempt to repel and disperse the attackers, to little avail. The apparent strength of his position was a chimera. Campbell's brilliant tactics forced the Loyalists to fight in the open on the summit while his own men were shielded on the slopes by trees and rocks. Picked off one at a time, Ferguson's men were steadily slaughtered. When the back-woodsmen gained the summit the end was at hand. The hated Scotsman tried to break out with some of his men but his body was pierced by multiple balls and he fell from his horse. Others tried to surrender, but screams of British atrocities rose from dozens of militia throats as they cut down, shot, and stabbed the helpless Loyalists. It took some time for sanity to return to King's Mountain.

The battle helped level the scale tipped so badly out of balance by the disaster at Camden. As the story goes, not a man escaped the hilltop inferno. Ferguson's losses were 225 killed, 163 wounded, and 716 captured, while Campbell suffered but 28 killed and 68 wounded. When Cornwallis received Ferguson's plea for help he dispatched Tarleton to assist him, but the cavalryman soon returned to Charlotte with word of the stunning disaster. Intelligence magnified Campbell's numbers to three thousand men. Recent sharp skirmishes, like the one that had greeted Cornwallis in Charlotte, confirmed an active and growing partisan threat from several quarters. The news gave even the offensive-minded Cornwallis pause. The important South Carolina posts of Ninety-Six and Camden, both well to his rear, were suddenly vulnerable.

Cornwallis turned the head of his army southward on October 14 and began what for him was the most painful withdrawal he had ever undertaken. The rainy and cold weather only added to his army's distress. Food was scarce and tents were in short supply. Illness swept the ranks, and even Cornwallis fell sick with fever and was forced to ride in the back of a slow moving wagon. The march took fif-teen miserable days to reach Winnsboro, South Carolina, a tiny crossroads hamlet sixty miles below Charlotte between Ninety-Six and Camden. Cornwallis encamped his army there and pondered his next move.

After the war Sir Henry Clinton gazed backward in time and recognized the hilltop battle for what it was. King's

Mountain, he lamented, "unhappily proved the first link in a chain of evils that followed each other in regular succession until they at last ended in the total loss of America." He was not far off the mark.

Meanwhile, many hundreds of miles to the north at West Point, New York, a general officer received a dispatch from George Washington dated the same day Cornwallis turned south for Winnsboro. Nathanael Greene was also about to head south.

*   *   *

The news from the southern colonies could not have been worse. So much had been expected of Horatio Gates's appointment in South Carolina that when news of his overwhelming defeat reached Congress many despaired of ever winning in that arena. Three men had been carefully chosen to lead there, and all three had come to grief. Now it was Nathanael Greene's turn. Could the Rhode Islander stand up against the unbeatable Cornwallis and wrest control of the Carolinas back from him? Even Greene was not entirely confident he would succeed. Still, he wrote, "I am not altogether without hopes of prescribing some bounds to the ravages of the enemy."

But with what would he fight Cornwallis? Gates was attempting to reorganize what was left of his army in Hillsboro, North Carolina, but only some hundreds of Continentals and a few squads of militia answered his call. Before he left for the long ride south Greene did his best to secure arms and supplies. He received promises of support from several Northern sources, including artillery, wagons, and $180,000 of practically worthless Continental paper. With the approach of winter he also knew that clothing would be in short supply. He advised Washington "to urge unceasingly the necessity of forwarding supplies for the southern army, as it will be impossible to carry on a winter campaign without clothing." Promises, largely of the empty variety, greeted both men. Delaware and Maryland excused themselves on the basis of "poverty" so pervasive that even forage for Greene's animals was considered impossible to supply.

By the end of November, Greene was in Hillsboro, and a few days later on December 2 he reined in his mount in Charlotte. Horatio Gates and his small mob of soldiery had been awaiting his arrival. It was an awkward meeting, but both men lived up to the moment. Greene, wrote one observer, met the disgraced Gates "with respectful sympathy and Gates, whose manners were those of a man of the world, returned his greeting with dignified politeness." Otho Williams, a veteran of the Camden debacle who would soon become one of Greene's most trusted lieutenants, recalled that the meeting was "an elegant lesson of propriety exhibited on a most delicate and interesting occasion." Gates issued an order turning over command to Greene on the following morning, remained for a few days to assist the new leader as best he could during the difficult transition, and then rode north. His military career, for all practical purposes, had reached an end.

If Washington's task in the northern colonies was difficult, Greene must have thought that his own mountain was all but unscalable. The army he commanded consisted of some fifteen hundred men. Fewer than one thousand were Continentals, and only about eight hundred were clothed and equipped to take the field. Only thin trickles of men were arriving each day. The appearance and condition of the army shocked Greene. My men, he wrote to a friend in January 1781, "[are] wretched beyond description, and their distress, on account of a lack of provisions, was little less than their suffering for want of clothing and other necessaries." Discipline had taken flight just as surely as General Gates had abandoned his army at Camden. The men were "so addicted to plundering that they were a terror to the inhabitants," lamented the new commander. Greene also had to move his camp because the area around

Charlotte had been divested of everything eatable. A new location was soon found some sixty miles to the southeast on the Pee Dee River near Cheraw Hill, where he was determined to repair his wagons, amass healthy horses, and discipline his semi-organized rabble.

Before he set out Greene signed an order that would flip the course of the war on its head in the south: he discarded one of the cardinal rules of war and determined to split his tiny army in the face of a superior and better equipped foe. This stunning move was the first of many he would make that used the strength and attributes of his British enemy against them. The genesis of this decision had its roots in the planned move to the Pee Dee River. Clearly he was not yet able to face Cornwallis on a pitched field of battle, but the last thing Greene needed was for others to interpret his relocation to a new encampment as a retreat. The situation called for partisan operations, and the division of the army would facilitate harassing tactics against both of Cornwallis's flanks. If the British general moved against either part of Greene's force, the other could threaten important British posts left undefended by the move. The two smaller armies would also be able to better subsist on their own, and their greater mobility would allow them to avoid being caught in a battle by the slower and more heavily laden enemy. Consequently, the army was cleaved in two.

On December 20, Greene moved to the new camp on the Pee Dee with General Isaac Huger's section, about eleven hundred Continental and militia infantry. The second and more mobile segment, about six hundred infantry and cavalry, was led by newly minted Brigadier General Daniel Morgan. Greene could not have made a better selection. The 45-year old officer was, as one historian noted, "a living legend" along the lines of a Davy Crockett or Daniel Boone. He was also one of the finest combat leaders fielded during the Revolution. Morgan's origins are obscure, but we know he was born in New Jersey to Welsh parents.

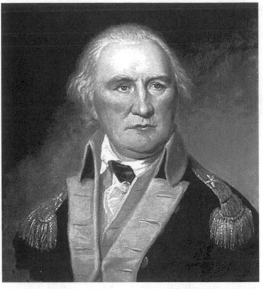

General Daniel Morgan.

After little if any schooling he left home as a teenager and struck out on his own for Pennsylvania and eventually Virginia. As a wagoner (and general rabble-rouser) he evacuated General Braddock's wounded during the French and Indian War. The five hundred lashes he earned as payment for a physical quarrel with a British officer did little to endear him to the rulers of Colonial America. Morgan saw his first formal action as a mounted ranger when he and a small group were set upon by musket-wielding Indians while carrying dispatches to Fort Edwards. A ball entered his neck and exited his mouth, knocking out many of his teeth in the process. His companion was killed. The determined Morgan remained in the saddle, outpaced his pursuers, and reached the fort. After the war he married and started family, continued hauling supplies for merchants, and settled down a bit. War was in his blood, however. Despite the beating he had received at the hands of the British, he donned a uniform in 1774 and experienced months of hard service for the Crown against the Shawnee in Ohio during the brief and all but forgotten Lord

Dunmore's War. Shortly thereafter a combat of a different sort broke over the land.

The 1775 explosions at Lexington and Concord convinced Morgan it was time to fight against the British, and he was quickly elected captain of a Virginia rifle company. Solid service in the operations around Boston and in Quebec followed, where he was captured. After his exchange in January 1777, Morgan transferred to Washington's army as a colonel and commander of five hundred light infantrymen, whom he led against Sir Howe's army in New Jersey. In the summer of 1777 Washington dispatched him north to join General Gates for the campaign against John Burgoyne. Morgan's stellar service there, word of which quickly spread across the colonies, played a substantial factor in Gates's final victory at Saratoga. After he returned to Washington's army Morgan quarreled with Congress over a promotion to brigadier general, tendered his resignation, and rode for home in the summer of 1779. Gates asked him to join the southern army the following spring, but his arthritis and painful sciatica (and personal anger at Congress) stood in the way. His patriotism ran deep, however, and proved more powerful than his resentment against the lawmakers. In August 1780 he remounted his horse with some difficulty and set out for Hillsboro, North Carolina. Gates had suffered his disastrous defeat at Camden, and the cause needed his help. Two months later Congress finally got around to promoting Morgan to brigadier general. He spent the next pair of months scouting for Gates, and on December 3, 1780, the same day Greene officially took command of the southern army, Morgan rode into Charlotte. He rode out again on December 21, moving westward with about one-third of Greene's puny army.

Morgan's orders were straightforward; the difficulty was in their execution. He was to pass over the Catawba River, join up with some North Carolina militia, gather supplies, and harass the enemy as strongly as possible. You may operate "either offensively or defensively, as your own prudence and discretion may direct," wrote Greene, "acting with caution and avoiding surprises by every possible precaution." His command consisted of three hundred and twenty Regulars from Maryland and Delaware, two hundred Virginia discharged Continentals, and about seventy-five light dragoons. North Carolina militia numbering about three hundred strong joined his army sixty miles west of Charlotte.

*　　*　　*

The approaching new year found Cornwallis in an agitated state. His planned move into North Carolina had been frustrated by Ferguson's sharp defeat at King's Mountain, and now Nathanael Greene, a competent commander familiar to him from several northern battlefields, had replaced Gates and promptly divided his army. Why would he violate every rule of war by doing so? Greene was not Horatio Gates, and clearly he was not a fool. Colonel Tarleton saw it as a terrible blunder waiting only for Cornwallis to move forward quickly and overwhelm him. Cornwallis, however, saw it for what it really was: a wise and calculated move based upon the realities of Greene's situation. His response was to sever his own recently reinforced army of four thousand men into three pieces. General Alexander Leslie, newly arrived from the north with twenty-five hundred infantry, would hold Camden against any American attack. Cornwallis, meanwhile, would slowly move north and west with the second chunk of his army in search of an opportunity to catch and defeat either Greene or what was left of Morgan after his third detachment under Banastre Tarleton finished with the "Old Waggoner."

The officer selected by Cornwallis to destroy Morgan seemed perfect for the job. His intended victim was almost twenty years old when Banastre Tarleton was born in 1754

Banastre Tarleton.

in Liverpool, England. Unlike Morgan's lineage, Tarleton came from upper middle class parents who saw to it he was properly educated at the universities at Liverpool and Oxford, where he studied law. He proved a wastrel when he squandered in less than one year a fortune left by his deceased father. Eager to participate in the coming war in America, the dashing and darkly handsome young man induced his mother to buy him a cavalry officer's commission in 1775 in the King's Dragoon Guards, the First Regiment of the Green Dragoons. After service around Charleston, Tarleton sailed north with Cornwallis, where his aggressive and capable handling of men soon brought him to the attention of his superiors. By August of 1778, the twenty-four-year-old Tarleton was a lieutenant colonel and one of the rising stars of the British army. He was also the new commander of a British legion comprised of cavalry and light infantry. "Tarleton's Legion" was almost entirely composed of American Loyalists from the middle colonies. Within a few months it was one of the best-trained and equipped units in America. It would play a prominent part in one of the war's most crushing British defeats.

The Liverpool native's outstanding service in almost every major engagement in the north was rewarded with a promotion to lead the British cavalry during Sir Clinton's southern campaign. His energetic service in the capture of Charleston included a sharp victory at Monck's Corner, followed up by one of the most contentiously debated small actions of the war at Waxhaws, South Carolina, on May 29, 1780. There, Tarleton's Legion attacked and annihilated a small American column ineptly led by Colonel Abraham Buford. Musket shots and the clanging of steel may have rung out for but a handful of minutes, but its controversial aftermath resounds to the present day. When the organized fighting ended men of the Legion continued cutting, slashing, stabbing, and shooting. Many walked among the wounded Americans and executed them. Rumors spread that the action took place under Tarleton's direct orders, and so Waxhaws gave rise to several nicknames for him, including "Ban the Butcher," and "Bloody Ban." Although Tarleton later denied the report, there is no doubt a massacre took place and that Tarleton may well have been the source of the order. The hated officer had helped surround and cut apart Gates's men at Camden later that summer, suffered through a long bout of illness when he was stricken with malaria, and recovered to fight in several sharp skirmishes and scouting actions. And then Cornwallis called upon him to catch and destroy Daniel Morgan.

Banastre Tarleton received his orders on New Year's Day in 1781. Cornwallis added a pair of infantry regiments to bolster his Legion and ordered him to maneuver Morgan in his direction so that the two British forces could corner and destroy him. "No time is to be lost," directed Cornwallis; to which Tarleton responded, "I must either destroy Morgan's corps or push it before me over Broad river toward King's

Mountain." He moved out north on January 15 with about eleven hundred men and two small field pieces, called "grasshoppers." Morgan had just slightly more than one thousand men, though Tarleton outnumbered him in Regulars by three to one. Cornwallis moved as well, though rain and mud slowed him down considerably.

Little slowed Tarleton down, however, and his aggressive raid soon caught up with Morgan. He drove so close his men enjoyed a hastily abandoned American breakfast. Worried that the British upstart might catch him at a disadvantage, Morgan took up camp and offered him battle at the Cowpens, South Carolina, just twenty miles southwest of King's Mountain. When Tarleton learned that his opponent was waiting in a piece of ground used to graze livestock, he ordered reveille blown early on January 17. By 3:00 A.M. his men were on the march in search of a victory.

A depiction of the battle of the Cowpens in South Carolina, January 17, 1781.

A victory was the last thing Morgan was going to give the hated Tarleton. The crusty Virginian had designed a plan of battle that was both ingenious and utterly original. Just as Nathanael Greene was learning all he could about Cornwallis's personality and tendencies, so too did Morgan listen carefully for the same purpose to those of his men who has faced Tarleton in the Carolinas. Both British officers favored hard and fast frontal assaults, and neither had a favorable view of Colonial militia. In what is now a legendary several hours, Morgan spent the night of January 16 and early morning hours of the 17th shifting from campfire to campfire, methodically explaining to his militiamen exactly what he expected of them.

That morning Morgan deployed his small army for battle. About one hundred and twenty handpicked marksmen from Georgia and North Carolina took position in the timber to shoot British officers. Behind them about one hundred and fifty yards were Andrew Pickens's men, another three hundred Carolina and Georgia militia, with another one hundred or so Virginia riflemen on their right. Morgan's principal force was positioned on a small rise another one hundred and fifty yards to the rear, where some three hundred Maryland and Delaware Regulars and the two hundred ex-Continental Virginians waited in silence. Out of sight behind the ridge was a reserve force of another one hundred and twenty-five infantry and cavalry. The crafty Morgan rode along his advance line, instructing his men to pick off the officers and then fall back to the line behind them. Morgan told Pickens's shaky militia to wait until the enemy approached to within fifty yards before firing two shots, after which they could retreat behind to the left rear and form there alongside the Continentals. The disposition was most unusual but would prove most effective.

The unsuspecting Tarleton arrived on the scene just before dawn. Reports revealed the terrain to be open and undulating, populated by sparse growths of trees largely free of underbrush—perfect for cavalry operations. A few miles behind Morgan ran the Broad River, and two creeks ran beyond his flanks, though too far away for him to anchor upon. He also knew most of Morgan's men were militia. Tarleton could not have been more delighted. Oblivious to the waiting trap he rode directly into Morgan's web.

It was a cold morning when the van of Tarleton's column of about eleven hundred men marched out of a body of trees and into the sight of the waiting American skirmishers. It was just short of 7:00 A.M. Fifty dragoons were ordered forward to disperse the pesky sharpshooters, and within a few minutes only thirty-five of them returned to their lines. Tarleton ordered about six hundred infantrymen to form and advance, leaving the balance behind as a reserve. Morgan's sharpshooters fell back as ordered. Pickens's militia, meanwhile, nervously held their fire until they could unleash a ragged but deadly volley in the face of the advancing infantry. The redcoats loosed an erratic fire in return that dropped only a handful of the militia, who quickly took the opportunity to scamper backward as planned to the main line. Tarleton had seen this before at Camden: the enemy was in retreat. The British dragoons charged and were sharply repulsed. A perturbed Tarleton ordered his infantry forward. They advanced but were stopped by the main line of Continentals, who stood tall and traded volleys with their British counterparts.

Morgan, meanwhile, gathered together masses of fleeing militia and guided them back to the right side of his line. The battle was barely thirty minutes old when Tarleton threw in his reserves in a last-ditch attempt to flank left and break Morgan's line. Instead it was they who broke when Morgan's line opened on them at short distance, followed by a rare American bayonet charge. Morgan's other men flanked the advanced enemy and the British Regulars ran from the field. Tarleton could not believe his eyes, and though he did his best the day could not be saved. He himself almost fell in hand-to-hand fighting and barely escaped with his life. The battle ended at 8:00 A.M. It had taken Morgan but sixty minutes to inflict the worst defeat any British army would suffer on an American battlefield.

Redcoat losses were heavy. Tarleton lost 110 killed, among them 39 officers. Prisoners included 230 wounded and some 600 unhurt—or about 85 percent of his effective force. Both "grasshoppers" were also lost, as were a pair of regimental standards, hundreds of muskets, dozens of wagons, and scores of horses. Morgan's losses were a paultry dozen killed and sixty wounded. The difference between a Morgan victory and a Tarleton success was obvious when Morgan refused to allow his men to slaughter the British in return for the bloodletting at Waxhaws. More important was the battle's aftermath. The news electrified every colony, heartened Greene and his men, and subtracted from Cornwallis his valuable and fast-moving light troops. More personal was the effect on Tarleton's career. Though he would continue to fight until the end of the war, the defeat cast a shadow that darkened his record forever.

One can only wonder what thoughts coursed through the brash Tarleton's mind as he rode his horse into the Turkey Creek encampment of Cornwallis to tell him his army had been involuntarily trimmed by one-quarter. According to one account, which may be apocryphal—but certainly not impossible—the shocked Cornwallis leaned on his sword with its tip embedded in the ground and listened to the report until the blade snapped in two. Although Cornwallis immediately pledged to recapture the prisoners, how he would do so remained to be seen. Reports had Morgan moving away from the battlefield and crossing the Catawba River. Tarleton demonstrated a modicum of professional honor by asking that he be allowed to retire and await a court of inquiry. Cornwallis refused. He needed every man in the field. Cowpens surely was a fluke, and not soon, if ever, to be repeated.

Cornwallis had planned a North Carolina campaign to catch either Morgan or Greene (or both), and he was determined to forge ahead with it. On January 18 he wrote to Sir Clinton that "nothing but the most absolute necessity shall induce me to give up the important object of the Winter's Campaign." Clinton, it will be recalled, had specifically instructed that Cornwallis not undertake any campaign that might jeopardize the dearly purchased real estate of South Carolina and Georgia. Clinton, however, was far away to the north, and Cornwallis was bound and determined to strike his enemy a blow—orders be damned. While Cornwallis was seeking a replacement sword, reinforcements in the form of General Leslie and fourteen hundred mixed Regular and militia infantry marched into camp from Camden. The army he took with him numbered about three thousand of all arms, half of whom were British or German Regulars.

Cornwallis struck out after Morgan on January 19 and floundered about on the wrong road for two days before picking up the American's scent. Morgan surprised Cornwallis by moving almost one hundred miles in just five days over roads that were all but impassable. His army was now on the east side of a rising Catawba River. Cornwallis was not going to catch old Dan Morgan any time soon. On January 25 at Ramsour's Mills, North Carolina, Cornwallis faced a gut-wrenching decision. He could no longer feed his animals and drive his slow-moving wagons fast enough to conduct a proper campaign. Rains, mud, wind, and poor roads had seen to that. But he was not about to turn back. Such a move was not in the makeup of the man. Instead, a giant fire was prepared and everything that could not be carried away was consumed by the flames. It was as if the ghost of Hernando Cortez had gained his ear. The army's tents, extra clothing, nonessential baggage, and supplies went up in smoke. Cornwallis had paved the way by destroying his own superfluous items, a move designed to compel his officers to act likewise. The fires even feasted upon most of the wheeled vehicles, whose essential contents were then loaded onto the backs of his men. The loss at Cowpens of Tarleton's light infantry and fast moving dragoons was coming home to haunt both "Ban the Butcher" and his beleaguered superior.

*   *   *

Morgan may have been elated by his victory over the hated Tarleton, but his own physical condition disgusted him. He could no longer sit in his saddle; arthritis and sciatica had laid the old soldier low. "I grow worse every hour," he wrote Nathanael Greene in a message dated January 24. "I cant ride out of a walk. I am exceedingly sorry to leave the field at such a time as this, but it must be the case. [Andrew] Pickens is an enterprising man and a very judicious one; perhaps he might answer the purpose." Two days later he wrote Greene again a very prescient observation: "I am convinced Cornwallis will push on til he is stopd by a force able to check him. I will do everything in my power but you may not put too much dependence on my, for I cant ride or walk." At this time Morgan had no knowledge that Cornwallis had burned his wagons and baggage to do exactly what Morgan had surmised he might.

An elated Greene learned of the stunning Cowpens victory on January 25. Cornwallis would not remain idle long after such a drubbing. For a time, Greene considered striking south against Ninety-Six, but the expiration of the enlistment of hundreds of Virginia militia bled his army as effectively as a battle, forcing him to abandon the idea. What to do? Strategic inspiration arrived with word on January 27 that Cornwallis had burned his wagons. The enemy was coming after Greene come hell or high water, a certainty that sparked a brilliant plan in the Rhode Islander's fertile mind. He would unite his army and withdraw slowly northward, keeping in front of Cornwallis but harassing him all the while. By doing so Greene hoped to lead the pugnacious British officer on a harrowing goose chase as far away as possible from his base of supplies and reinforcements. The inclement weather and bad roads would do the rest, wearing down the British army and weakening its morale until a suitable time arrived to turn and give battle. Greene's line of supply, meanwhile, would shorten as he moved north closer to his supply outlets in Virginia, from which point any reinforcements would also have to arrive. Now he just had to avoid Cornwallis and yet remain close enough to give that general hope of a victory. It was both a bold and difficult plan and, except for George Washington, no one other than Nathanael Greene was capable of pulling it off.

Greene also decided to ride and see Morgan, who was tending to a few important matters before heading home. While Isaac Huger's wing of the army at Cheraw fell back into North Carolina to a position along the Yadkin River near Salisbury, Greene rode through Tory-infested lands for 125 miles with but a handful of guards to join the Old Waggoner on the Catawba. He reached him on January 30. Morgan apparently disagreed with Greene's plan and wanted instead to fall back into the mountains. Greene would have none of it. Cornwallis was the objective. When Morgan confirmed the destroyed baggage and intelligence that the general intended to march north, Greene shouted, "Then, he is ours!" Partisan captains were ordered to bring in their bands and join the army. To the Swamp Fox known as Francis Marion, Greene wrote, "Here is a fine field and great glory ahead." An adamant Morgan, perhaps still in pain, condemned Greene's strategy and told him that he would not be responsible for the ill consequences he was certain would flow from it. "Neither will you," replied Greene, who showed all the hallmarks of a great captain by standing strong in the face of such prominent opposition. "I shall take the measure upon myself."

And so the plan developed. Rain had swollen the Catawba River sufficiently to temporarily hold back Cornwallis. Morgan's men would march on the road to the

Yadkin River and unite with Huger's men while General William Davidson's eight hundred militiamen guarded the several river fords to contest the crossings and hold back the British as long as possible.

Cornwallis came close to stopping Greene's plan before it began. The rain stopped and the river began falling on January 31. In an effort to bag Morgan, Cornwallis led his army in a two-pronged flanking operation across the Catawba early on the morning of February 1. He was too late, for Morgan had left his camp the previous day and his men were now thirty miles away. The crossing downriver at Cowan's Ford, however, was hotly contested and British losses were almost certainly sharply higher than Cornwallis's admitted forty killed and wounded. But he was now across the river. Tarleton's men, meanwhile, rode quickly inland several miles to Torrence Tavern, where they inflicted a stinging defeat upon Davidson's retreating militiamen. Among the dead was Davidson himself.

Nathanael Greene was but six miles away with a small guard at this time awaiting the arrival of the militia when word reached him of the skirmish and Davidson's death. Cornwallis was now on the wrong side of the Catawba and Tarleton was prowling about in the neighborhood. Without sparing a moment he mounted his horse, set his spurs, and rode off. Several miles later he stopped at a roadside inn, where someone who knew him inquired, "What, alone, Greene?" He answered in the affirmative, "Yes, alone, tired, hungry, and penniless." When the innkeeper's wife heard his response, she carried out two small bags of coin and handed them to him. "You need this more than I do," she told him. As one historian of the war noted, "The contents of these two little bags constituted the entire military chest of the Grand Army of the Southern Department of the United States of America."

* * *

With Cornwallis over the Catawba River the pace of the campaign entered a more active and dangerous phase for both participants. Ahead of both armies were two major rivers—the Yadkin and the Dan. Between them were innumerable tributaries, spider-like creeks, and seemingly endless swamp land. By February 3 the British were in Salisbury, with Greene's men a mere eight miles away on the far side of the flooded Yadkin. Cornwallis pondered his options until learning that the lower (or more eastern) fords on the Dan River, which ran along the North Carolina and Virginia border, were passable only with an armada of boats. The information was critical, for if he could cut Greene off from the Dan's upstream (or more western) crossing points, he could trap him below the river and cut him to pieces.

The next day Cornwallis learned that Greene and Morgan were marching north, which probably confirmed Cornwallis's conviction that his opponent's objective was the upper crossing points. He promptly swung his own army north and crossed the Yadkin ten miles upstream at Shallow Ford on February 8 before making a beeline northeast to effect his strategy. He was now closer to the upper fords than Greene. Unbeknownst to Cornwallis, however, Greene did indeed plan to cross the Dan—but not upstream. He had already ordered the gathering and building of boats many miles downstream, something Cornwallis had no way of knowing. Beyond the Dan, hoped Greene, were the supplies and extra men he so desperately needed.

While Cornwallis was striking at air Greene was turning east. He camped on February 6 at a small crossroads hamlet called Guilford Courthouse. Huger's division met up with them there, and the army was finally united for the first time in weeks. Huger's infantrymen were "in a most dismal condition for want of clothing, especially shoes, being obliged to march, the chief part of them, barefoot from Cheraw Hills," remembered one observer. Greene took special notice of the terrain around the courthouse

Colonel Otho Williams.

and seriously considered offering Cornwallis battle there, but when the expected reinforcements and ammunition did not arrive he changed his mind. His entire army numbered but two thousand men, with only fourteen hundred of these Regulars. Greene's intelligence told him that Cornwallis marched with upward of thirty-five hundred well-equipped and trained veterans. Instead of fighting Cornwallis, Greene detached hundreds of men to harass the enemy and lead him north and west toward the upper fords while Greene and Huger headed north and east for the downstream crossing points.

It was at this time that Dan Morgan left the army for good. Unable to remain in the field, the redoubtable warrior retired to Virginia, his military life at an end. His men were turned over to Otho Williams, in whose good hands they would remain. Greene would miss the surly old warrior very soon.

The race for the Dan, some seventy miles to the north, pressed relentlessly onward. Otho Williams and hundreds of light infantry and cavalry led Cornwallis on a wild and exhausting march that included several bloody clashes and close calls too numerous to count. Williams, however, remained just out of reach which irked an already irate Cornwallis no end. Finally, on February 15, a courier reached Williams with a message from Greene: "All our troops are over and the stage is clear. . . . I am ready to receive you and give you a hearty welcome." The cheers that coursed through the American ranks were so loud that the forward elements of Cornwallis's army, miles away, heard the shouting. Every British and Hessian foot soldier knew what they meant.

The crisis, at least for the moment, had passed.

* * *

Lord Cornwallis was outraged at being duped, but he had also swept Greene completely out of North Carolina. No organized army remained in the deep south, but what exactly had he won? His own army had suffered some two hundred and fifty losses to wounds, illness, and desertion. He could not cross north of the river without boats, and he was now deep inside a completely stripped enemy territory with his own supply base more than two hundred miles to the south. He could not remain where he was, and falling back would dishearten the Loyalists and inspire the damnable Colonialists. If the thought crossed his mind, and it surely must have, the parallel to his own situation with that of General John Burgoyne's in upstate New York earlier in the war must have been more than unsettling. Out of viable options, an embittered Cornwallis rested his men for one day and then began a more leisurely march southward to Hillsboro.

Greene, too, found himself in a rather odd situation. He had saved his own army and exhausted his opponent's in a skilled withdrawal against a cagey veteran, but campaigns are not won by deep retreats. Now was the time to turn upon Cornwallis, but the reinforcements Greene expected had failed to materialize. His problems were compounded by the expiring enlistments of his own militia, most of whom had left for home. His army, in all its glory, numbered no more than fifteen hundred men. If he did not find a way to strike a blow against Cornwallis soon, all of his effort would have been in vain. When news reached him that Cornwallis was heading south, Greene dispatched a force of cavalry and infantry below the falling Dan River on February 18 to harass the withdrawal. Two days later Otho Williams and his veterans were also dispatched with similar orders. Three days later, after Greene was pleasantly pleased by the appearance of six hundred Virginia militia under General Edward Stevens, he slipped the rest of his army south of the Dan and moved once more into North Carolina. His plan was little changed: he would grind down Cornwallis with piecemeal partisan hit-and-run tactics, holding him as far from his supply base as possible, while simultaneously working to keep Tory recruitment at minimal levels.

Cornwallis, meanwhile, knew he could not long remain at Hillsboro, where food and forage were all but unobtainable. On February 27 he crossed the Haw River and marched his men southwest and made camp along Alamance Creek at the intersection of several important roads. The eastern route led to Hillsboro, and a southeasterly road led in the direction of coastal Wilmington, one of his primary supply bases. The road north and west led to Guilford Courthouse. The next day Greene and much of his army also went into camp at Speedwell Ironworks, about thirty miles above the British position in the forks of Deep River.

Both armies spent the next ten days moving a few miles in one direction and then back again, feinting here and there in an effort to deceive the other. A sharp skirmish erupted at Wetzell's Mill on March 6 and the blood of a few dozen men was shed, but Cornwallis's attempt to catch Greene in a decisive battle was yet again unsuccessful. Cornwallis's aggressive streak had not abated.

And then what Greene had long awaited and yearned for

came to pass. Over the next few weeks thousands of men
seeped into his army. Some four hundred Continentals
from Virginia arrived with Colonel Richard Campbell, as
did one thousand and sixty North Carolina militia in two
brigades under Brigadier General John Butler and Colonel
Thomas Eaton. Two more brigades of Virginia militia, some
nearly seventeen hundred strong, crowded into camp.
Greene was elated. He also knew that the time to fight had
arrived. He could not expect to augment his strength much
more than the forty-four hundred men he now had under
arms, his new militia would only fight for another six
weeks, and his commissary had stripped the surrounding
region clean. Battle beckoned, and the right ground was
close at hand. On March 12 his men packed two days'
rations and tramped about eighteen miles south to
Guilford Courthouse in a bid to smoke out Cornwallis.

The climax of the campaign was at hand. If Cornwallis
destroyed Greene as he had Gates, he could easily move his
army into Virginia and the war in the southern colonies, for
all practical purposes, would be over. If Greene, however,
whipped Cornwallis this far from his base of supply, the
entire complexion of the war would be altered in a single
day. Everyone on both sides of the Atlantic with an interest
in the ongoing campaign had been following it as closely as
the slow-moving communications of the day had allowed.

The stakes were high and the last cards were about to be
dealt.

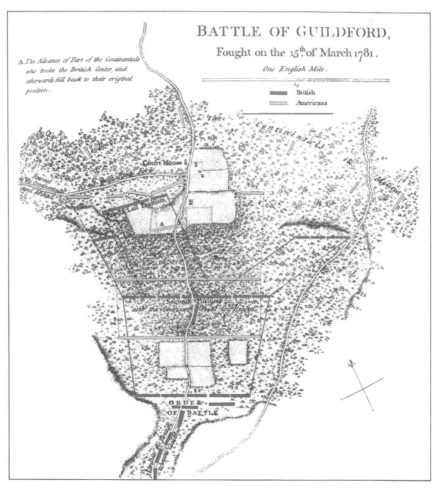

BATTLE OF GUILDFORD,

Fought on the 15th of March 1781.

This map was published in 1787 in Lt. Col. Banastre Tarleton's *Campaigns of 1780 and 1781 in the Southern Provinces of North America*. It was based on a map drawn in the field by one of Cornwallis's army engineers.

CHAPTER 4

THE BATTLE OF GUILFORD COURTHOUSE: THE FIRST LINE

"If they [militia] fight, you will beat Cornwallis; if not, he will beat you, and perhaps cut your regulars to pieces."—Daniel Morgan

THE ARMY NATHANAEL GREENE CARRIED with him to Guilford Courthouse was sizeable in numbers, but top heavy with militia. Careful deployment and a solid performance from everyone would be necessary to defeat the experienced enemy he hoped would soon be closing on him.

Cornwallis learned what worked well in the field, and so did Greene, who took heed of his own and others' successes and failures. He had witnessed time and again on northern fields that untried militia could not be expected to face down and volley with British Regulars, let alone stand and take a determined bayonet attack. Camden had proven the same recipe was true in the lower colonies. On his way home Daniel Morgan had written Greene about that very matter. "If they [militia] fight, you will beat Cornwallis; if not, he will beat you, and perhaps cut your regulars to pieces." His observation was tempered with sound but hard advice: "Put the militia in the center, and with some picked troops in their rear, with orders to shoot down the first man that runs."

Although Greene ignored Morgan's last recommendation, he decided to deploy his militia as the ailing general suggested—in the center with picked men in their rear and on their flanks. Daniel Morgan had unlocked the key to using militiamen at his stunning Cowpens victory, and Greene was smart enough to use that fight as his general blueprint for victory at Guilford Courthouse.

If Cornwallis took the bait he would approach the field of battle from the south and west along the New Garden (or Great Salisbury Wagon) Road. The narrow dirt track—for it was little more than that—ran generally southwest to northeast, beginning low and rising in elevation as it neared the courthouse crossroads. It was surrounded on both sides by undulating hills covered with trees and brush. It was perfect for what the Rhode Islander had in mind.

Greene ordered his army to take position in three lines perpendicular to the New Garden Road. His least trust-worthy militia comprised two regiments of North Carolina foot, about 1,060 men under the command of Brigadier General John Butler and Colonel Thomas Eaton. The for-mer's men were predominantly from Granville, Guilford, and Orange counties, while the latter's hailed from the counties of Halifax and Warren. They took up a position along the southwestern side of a skirt of timber behind a split-rail fence facing an open field about one-quarter of a mile square. They had a clear field of fire all the way to the defile where the road snaked out of the woods four hun-dred yards away. There is some debate as to who was posi-tioned where, but General Butler, who commanded his state's Hillsboro military district, seems to have formed his men on the right flank, west of the New Garden Road while Eaton's militia mimicked the procedure on the left side, or east of the track. Both of their flanks extended off out of sight into the woods. Neither man had much if any experience in the field, and both were political appointees. Two six-pounders under the able command of Captain Anthony Singleton were wheeled up and rolled into posi-tion on the road between the regiments.

William Richardson Davie, the same North Carolina offi
cer who had so warmly greeted the head of Cornwallis's
column when he had rashly poked it inside Charlotte's
town limits, was now serving as Greene's quartermaster.
Davie did not think much of the ground chosen for his fellow North Carolinians. "It was certainly a great mistake to
draw up the militia to await the attack of regular troops for
several hours, and the position of the front line was actually advantageous to the Enemy, the elevated grounds
enabled them to display with order and despatch, and a
common rail fence behind which about half the No.
Carolina Militia were posted was a cover too insignificant
to inspire any confidence, the rest of the line was as much
exposed as any Troops could be in the woods."

According to Henry "Light-Horse Harry" Lee, these back
country men were rugged and tough, though he exaggerated quite a bit when he added that they "never alarmed at
meeting with equal numbers of British infantry." In fact
they almost always panicked at the sight of approaching
redcoats, which is why Morgan had advised Greene to
place reliable men on their flanks. This Greene wisely did.

On Butler's right flank were two hundred Virginia riflemen, veterans to a man, under the command of Colonel
Charles Lynch. William Washington's dragoons, who numbered close to one hundred were also there, as was Captain
Robert Kirkwood's company of eighty elite Continental
infantry of the vaunted Delaware Line. Eaton's left flank
below the road was similarly supported. Colonel William
Campbell's two hundred rifles both lengthened the line
and added battle-hardened experience in that quarter.
Henry "Light-Horse Harry" Lee's mixed legion of seventy-
five cavalry and eight-two infantrymen, which was cur-
rently away on other duty, would soon take up a position
there as well. Such was the composition of the American
first line of battle.

The second line was arranged with similar care about 350
yards behind the first, with the road again serving as the

dividing line. There were two primary differences between this position and the North Carolina line. The men were aligned atop a gentle but noticeable ridge, and timber completely concealed the twelve hundred or so Virginians who had formed there. They, too, were largely untrained and untried militia, but unlike their North Carolina comrades, a healthy scattering of these men and officers were discharged Continental soldiers, and so had experienced the scent of gunpowder smoke on a field of battle. Some of these officers and men also had experience fighting against Indians. The Virginians were organized into two 600-man brigades. One was led by Brigadier General Robert Lawson and the other by Brigadier General Edward Stevens. There is ample confusion in the sources as to where these men deployed. "Light-Horse Harry" Lee specifically states that "they were formed in a deep wood; the right flank of Stevens and the left flank of Lawson resting on the great [New Garden] road." In other words, Stevens held the left and Lawson the right. The course of events clearly supports this supposition. Lawson's men were drawn mainly from Virginia's southside counties, such as Pittsylvania, Prince Edward, Cumberland, and Amelia. They had little, if any, experience in the war thus far. Lawson himself had commanded a Continental regiment, "but had been left without troops by the compression of our corps," explained one officer. Lawson's fellow brigadier had an even more impressive resume.

Edward Stevens was a native of Culpeper, Virginia, where he was born in 1745. He would die there as well, though not for another thirty-nine years. Unlike many of his men, he had a substantial amount of military experience, first as a battalion commander of militia at the skirmish of Great Bridge in December 1775, and again in 1777 as colonel of the 10th Virginia Regiment, which he had crisply led in a blocking movement in New Jersey in 1777 against Sir William Howe's Regulars along Brandywine Creek. Competent service followed again at Germantown, after which Congress promoted him to brigadier general. Much of the credit he had earned throughout the war was wiped away by a single piece of advice he provided Horatio Gates in August of 1780. As the leader of seven hundred militia, he urged that incompetent recreant to engage the approaching British army outside Camden, apparently believing (wrongly) that it was too late to retreat. When the British moved against him Stevens's men ran away almost immediately, most without firing so much as a single round. The men now standing with him hailed from the western Virginia "rifle counties" of Rockbridge, Augusta, and Rockingham. In an attempt to avoid another embarrassment, Stevens handpicked forty men and placed them behind his line with orders to shoot down anyone who left his post without orders to do so. He had a lot of ground to make up at Guilford Courthouse.

The strength of Greene's defense-in-depth strategy rested in his powerful third line of battle, which was taken up about five hundred yards behind and to the right (or west) of the Virginians. Here were to be found the American Regulars, fourteen hundred strong from Virginia, Delaware, and Maryland. Their line was entirely above the New Garden Road on a commanding piece of open high ground not far from the courthouse that provided the crossroads with its name. A checkerboard of open fields sloped down and away from the front of the third line south and west into a bowl-shaped cleared valley. It was the best defensive position on the entire battlefield, with timber behind it, open fields of fire to the front, and a steep ridge that would prevent any turning movement against the far left flank. About a hundred yards behind the line was the Reedy Fork Road, the army's primary route of escape should such a thing become necessary. The primary New Garden Road angled away north and east from the courthouse crossroads to Speedwell Furnace on Troublesome Creek, halfway to the Dan River crossings and the Virginia state line.

Isaac Huger's (pronounced you-gee) Virginia Brigade of two regiments held the right wing of the third line. Like General Stevens in the line ahead of him, Huger had also blundered badly at a place called Monck's Corner. Unlike Stevens, Huger did not enjoy a resume as rich with military experience. On Huger's left was the army's second pair of six-pounder cannons under the command of Captain Samuel Finley, followed by the Maryland Brigade, whose men were in the capable hands of Colonel Otho Holland Williams. His 1st and 2nd Maryland Regiments were capably led by, respectively, Colonel John Gunby (whose regiment contained a company of Delaware veterans) and Lieutenant Colonel Benjamin Ford. The far left flank of Ford's Maryland outfit bent back near the New Garden Road and ran east along it for a short distance, forming a shallow L-shaped configuration. If members of the 1st Maryland Regiment boasted of being the finest such outfit on the continent, few would raise eyebrows in disbelief. They were the best men Greene ever fielded. The Delaware men, too, had enjoyed long and exceptional field experience. Huger's men, however, could boast of no such record. They had been raised only a year earlier to replace troops lost in the surrender of Charleston in 1780. Though they were not nearly as seasoned as their brethren to the left, their discipline was tight and their morale high. They were, after all, Continentals.

And so Greene's dispositions were now complete. Clearly he had little confidence in the ability of his militia to stand and fight. Rather, his desire was to wear down the enemy with the expendable militia before Cornwallis's veterans came into contact with his small and coveted force of Continentals. This fact was not lost on some of the militia officers. As the always perceptive General Davie observed, "General Greene by the Disposition of his Troops does not appear to have conceived the design of conquering but crippling Lord Cornwallis. His 2nd line was too remote from the 1st to give it any support, and the position of the continentals forbad any movement that could either succor the 2d line or second their efforts. That each division became stationary and Genl Greene appears to have calculated alone upon the impetuosity of Lord Cornwallis as the means of bringing his troops into action." Davie's assessment was absolutely correct.

Hours earlier, long before these men in these three lines had grown comfortable in their new positions, Greene had ordered Harry Lee and his Legion, together with William Campbell and a squad of Virginia riflemen, to advance into the dark countryside and determine whether Cornwallis was advancing. As Lee rode forward he cleaved off a detachment of dragoons under a Lieutenant James Heard with orders to conduct a deep scout and determine enemy intentions. About 2:00 A.M. a courier galloped back with news that "a large body of horse" was thundering in their direction. Tarleton was on the move! But was Cornwallis's infantry marching behind him? Greene ordered Lee to penetrate the British cavalry screen and find out. Passing around the flanks of Tarleton's horsemen, however, proved

Henry "Light-Horse Harry" Lee.

impossible. Heard did his best, but reported "having been uniformly interrupted by patrols ranging far from the British line of march." His men had also heard "the rumbling of wheels, which indicated a general movement." If true, Lord Cornwallis was tramping toward Guilford Courthouse, albeit slowly, conscious of the threat of an ambuscade in the darkness. Greene received the news without any outward show of emotion. It was exactly as he wished it to be. The sun was still an hour from rising when he ordered reveille blown and a quick breakfast cooked and devoured. If his men were going to fight this day, they would do so on full stomachs.

Uneasy about the report, Greene scribbled a message and passed it along to Lee, asking that he confirm the exact state of affairs in his front. The Virginian sprang into the saddle and moved down the road with riflemen deployed on either side should they run into more opposition than the horsemen alone could handle. They ran into Heard's returning men a couple miles to the front; Tarleton's troopers were following in their wake. It was dark and the narrow road was fringed with high and strongly built fences on both sides—perfect conditions for an ambush. Knowing well Tarleton's penchant for hit and run tactics, Lee ordered his horsemen in the rear to make haste and gallop away, while those in front, who would play the bait, withdrew at a more leisurely pace. Sensing an opportunity to catch and destroy a slow-moving segment of enemy cavalry was something "Ban the Butcher" would not easily pass up.

Lee was not disappointed. Within a few seconds Tarleton's cavalrymen drove forward for what they believed would be an easy kill. Lee waited until the last moment and then calmly ordered his troopers to turn quickly and charge at speed with their much larger and healthier mounts. The collision of thousands of pounds of horseflesh and swords in the narrow North Carolina lane could be heard from some distance away. As Lee described

Members of Henry Lee's Legion in action on the battlefield.

the action, "The whole of the enemy's section was dis-mounted, and many of the horses prostrated, some of the dragoons killed, the rest made prisoners. Not a single American soldier or horse was injured." Their obnoxious commander, he noted with delight, withdrew with celerity.

Bitten now by the same bug that always infected Tarleton, Lee made the same mistake and ordered a charge into the darkness to cut off the escaping enemy. Tarleton, however, slipped through a gap in the fencing "on an obscure way" and Lee's men thundered past, galloping into the rising light of day—and directly into a line of raised British muskets. The rising sun glinted on the polished barrels, confusing Lee's horse so much that he was forced to dismount his animal and jump onto the back of another. The Legion's troopers fell back amidst a hail of flying lead. Lee later maintained that "This fire was innocent, overshooting the cavalry entirely, whose caps and accouterments were all struck with green twigs, cut by the British ball out of the large oaks in the meeting-house yard, under which the cavalry received the volley from the guards." A brisk engagement of some thirty minutes duration opened between Lee's men with the Colonial infantry who had trotted forward to support them and the advance of Cornwallis's veteran army. The action, remembered one participant, "was bravely maintained on both sides" until the Americans withdrew.

The most prominent injury incurred during the sharp skirmish was suffered by Tarleton, who caught a musket ball in his right hand. The shot ripped apart his thumb and index finger and forced the vain officer to sling his arm for the balance of the fight. Within twenty-four hours a doctor would amputate both of them. Lee lost a few prisoners but reported his killed and wounded as "light." Tarleton, who routinely exaggerated his accomplishments and minimized his defeats, claimed that "Colonel Lee's dragoons retreated with precipitation along the main road, and Colonel Campbell's mountaineers were dispersed with considerable loss. The pursuit was not pushed far, as there were many proofs besides the acknowledgment of prisoners, that General Greene was at hand."

Losses were probably equally suffered, but now both men knew what they had set out to discover. "General

Greene being immediately advised of what had passed, prepared for battle," remembered Lee, "not doubting that the long avoided, now wished-for, hour was at hand."

*   *   *

Cornwallis had also been pining for this day to arrive. News had reached him the previous afternoon, March 14, that Greene had moved forward to a position about twelve miles distant near Guilford Courthouse. A few hours later the news was confirmed. Was he deploying in search of a battle, or merely maneuvering once more to keep him guessing? Cornwallis had not fought a single major action for weeks, but he had still lost about 17 percent of his army through illness, desertions, and wounds. His command hovered now at slightly less than two thousand of all arms. He estimated Greene had several times that number. Rations were low and getting lower. Both army commanders were feeling the pressure to fight or retire out of sheer necessity. Cornwallis had been desperately seeking a confrontation. Up until now, Greene had not.

Cornwallis sent off his remaining sick and baggage to Bell's Mills on Deep River under the protection of approximately two hundred men from Lieutenant Colonel John Hamilton's Royal North Carolina Regiment and a small force of cavalry. The rest of the army was issued ammunition and told to prepare for battle. The men would march before dawn. He would catch Greene early the next day while there was still enough sun in the sky to defeat him. Hours before the men moved out Tarleton fanned his legion out in advance to clear the countryside and protect the van of the army. The infantrymen stepped off in the cold darkness a good hour before morning's light.

The head of the long column of red, green, and blue uniformed men tramped silently in their ranks for only a short time when the sound of distant gunfire broke the heavy stillness of the night. Tarleton, reported a courier, had met enemy horsemen. Another mile was gained, and then another. The sounds of battle and running horses drew closer by the second. An officer history has not named calmly formed the light infantry of the Guards in a line across the road, ordered their muskets raised, and waited for the enemy to arrive. A cold dawn was just breaking, typical of a late winter day in the North Carolina piedmont. A volley was loosed in the direction of the American horsemen, followed by a tense engagement of some thirty minutes with Lee's men and some unknown force of Colonial infantry who had scampered forth to support him. It ended suddenly when the Americans melted away into the night. Cornwallis rode to the front and ordered Tarleton to press the retiring enemy.

Greene was asking for battle. He would have it. The column continued its march to Guilford Courthouse.

* * *

"Light-Horse Harry" Lee had rejoined the army and was busy placing his cavalry and foot soldiers on the far left flank of the first line of militia when Nathanael Greene made his appearance at the front. The British would soon emerge from the trees in the distance, and the harbingers of death, otherwise known to the soldiers as the fife and drum, would plainly be heard by all. The calm general dismounted and spoke gentle words of encouragement while walking his horse in front of the waiting and nervous Carolinians. The sun was well up and the general was sweating. He had good reason to sweat. One man remembered that he removed his hat and dabbed his ample forehead with his handkerchief. Greene reminded all within earshot why they were there this day and spoke of freedom and honor, dignity and family. "Two rounds, my boys, and then you may fall back!" he instructed them. "Just two rounds and then you may retire." Daniel Morgan had instructed his militia at Cowpens in the same manner with

Marker describing the action along Greene's first line of defense. The British army would have advanced up this road, which follows the route of the New Garden Road up to the bounds of the park.

Trail that follows the route of the New Garden Road as it traverses the park.

stunning success. Perhaps it would pay off today. With that the Rhode Islander who had staked everything on the day's outcome mounted his horse, turned its head northeast, and trotted away to the second line of battle.

Now it was "Light-Horse Harry" Lee's turn. The cavalier had spent much of the night harassing the approaching British. He was tired, but energized by the possibility of administering a drubbing on old Cornwallis. Though his yet-to-be born son, Robert Edward, would rise to a level of fame Henry could never imagine, and he would live after the war to disgrace his family, by 1781 Henry Lee was himself a household name. The blonde and blue-eyed Virginia native and Princeton University graduate had seen most of the war from the back of a horse. His service in the northern colonies had quickly garnered General Washington's attention—especially when his surprise attack at Paulus Hook, New Jersey, netted some four hundred British prisoners at the cost of but one American casualty. His adroit horsemanship earned him the nickname "Light-Horse Harry" and the thanks of Congress, which promoted him to major-commandant and rewarded him with a mixed independent command of horse and foot that would forever after be known as "Lee's Legion." His hit-and-run tactics in the southern colonies were renowned throughout the country. He was courageous, impetuous, and intelligent, and Nathanael Greene had come to depend on him for his keen reconnaissance abilities and steady hand. He was just twenty-five years old.

Lee guided his mount along the line of North Carolinians to say his piece. He was not as plain spoken or calm as the commanding general. Word of his unexpected appearance would have swept through the ranks of the admiring militia. Greene had conversed in moderated tones, but Lee let loose with a blistering sermon about how the British could be beaten and how Greene was just the man to do it. It was not yet 1:00 P.M. One of the men who heard Lee speak was Captain Richard Harrison of Granville County, North

Carolina. His wife Nancy was heavy with a child due that very day. On a scrap of dirty paper pulled from his jacket he scribbled a few hasty lines to this beloved woman. "It is scarcely possible to paint the agitations of my mind," he told her. "I am struggling with two of the greatest events that are in nature at the same time, the fate of my Nancy and my country. Oh my God," he concluded, "I trust them with thee; do with them for the best."

* * *

No one is exactly sure when the British arrived on the field at Guilford Courthouse. Some reports place it at noon, others at a more vague "midday." One modern source states that the head of the British column became visible to the North Carolinians "about 1:30 P.M."—the same time Cornwallis later claimed he actually opened the fighting. Nonetheless, arrive they did and in a fashion purposely designed to inflict as much mental anguish as possible on the knock-kneed American militia.

Riding near the van of his army, Cornwallis watched while the head of his column turned right and left into a cleared area near a few scattered buildings known locally as the Hoskins' farm. A line of the enemy was spotted about four hundred yards to the east behind a fence. A sharp crack followed by a puff of smoke erupted and a ball whizzed past into the woods beyond. Enemy artillery had opened fire. Cornwallis ordered up three guns of his own (some sources say they were six-pounders, and others three-pounders) under Lieutenant John McLeod of the Royal Artillery and a spirited duel unfolded while the infantry prepared for battle. The combative soldier who had experienced war on so many fields was willingly entering a battle on ground of his enemy's choosing without fully knowing either his strength or the lay of the land. "He had marched his army to rags," one historian has written, and he was not about to hesitate now. His oversights would prove costly.

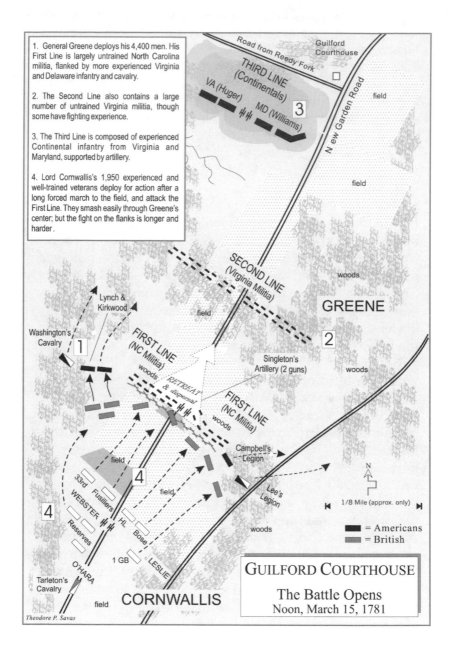

1. General Greene deploys his 4,400 men. His First Line is largely untrained North Carolina militia, flanked by more experienced Virginia and Delaware infantry and cavalry.

2. The Second Line also contains a large number of untrained Virginia militia, though some have fighting experience.

3. The Third Line is composed of experienced Continental infantry from Virginia and Maryland, supported by artillery.

4. Lord Cornwallis's 1,950 experienced and well-trained veterans deploy for action after a long forced march to the field, and attack the First Line. They smash easily through Greene's center; but the fight on the flanks is longer and harder.

Road from Reedy Fork

Guilford Courthouse

THIRD LINE (Continentals)

VA (Huger)

MD (Williams)

New Garden Road

field

field

SECOND LINE (Virginia Militia)

woods

GREENE

Lynch & Kirkwood

field

Washington's Cavalry

FIRST LINE (NC Militia)

woods

Singleton's Artillery (2 guns)

woods

RETREAT & dispersal

FIRST LINE (NC Militia)

woods

Campbell's Legion

33rd Fusiliers

WEBSTER

field

field

Lee's Legion

N

HL Bose

Reserves

woods

1/8 Mile (approx. only)

1 GB

LESLIE

= Americans
= British

Tarleton's Cavalry

O'HARA

GUILFORD COURTHOUSE

CORNWALLIS

field

The Battle Opens
Noon, March 15, 1781

Theodore P. Savas

It took Cornwallis about half an hour to prepare for battle. He deployed his army in two lines, with the left more heavily weighted. Colonel James Webster's command comprised the left front of the army. Immediately to the left (or west) of New Garden Road he placed the Royal Welsh (23rd Regiment) Fusiliers, with the 33rd Foot extending the line to the left with its own left flank brushing up against a thick stand of trees. Webster was Cornwallis's finest officer and one of the Crown's best field commanders. He was born in 1740, the second son of a prominent Edinburgh clergyman and occasional moderator of the General Assembly. Webster was commissioned lieutenant in 1760 and served with the 33rd Foot, Cornwallis's former regiment. Company command came his way as early as 1763 and the rank of major followed eight years later. Before the war broke out he was a lieutenant colonel and Colonel Lord Cornwallis was his immediate superior. Like Cornwallis, Webster carved out a proud military career in the colonies. Many credited the June 1777 Monmouth "victory" to his hard fighting and tight tactical leadership. Sir Henry Clinton referred to him as "that gallant officer," high praise from a man who normally reserved such acclaim for himself. Webster's service in the Southern colonies as an acting brigadier was also stellar and included numerous small unit actions and the engagement at Monck's Corner. His most conspicuous service was rendered on the field at Camden, where his amazing control over his brigade helped seal the doom of Gates's army. He was forty-one years old at Guilford Courthouse. He had nothing to prove to anyone.

Brigadier General Charles O'Hara's men deployed in a line of support behind Webster. His men included the 2nd Guards Battalion, a Grenadier company and a light infantry company of the Guards, and a company of German Jägers. The widely experienced O'Hara came rather late to the war in America, arriving in July 1778. When O'Hara arrived in the colonies Sir Clinton tapped

Reconstructed buildings of the Hoskins Farm in Tannenbaum Historic Park. Lord Cornwallis formed his troops for the battle of Guilford Courthouse on the grounds of the Hoskins Farm.

him to command at Sandy Hook, New Jersey, though he soon quickly found his personal habits distasteful. Two years later he was Brigadier General O'Hara and leader of the Brigade of Guards, Cornwallis's second-in-command, and quickly thereafter his fast friend. O'Hara's ability to drive men on the march had become obvious to all around him during the largely fruitless pursuit of Nathanael Greene to the Dan River. O'Hara's aggressive performance at Cowan's Ford the previous month had been exemplary. Exactly how he would perform at the head of his men in a pitched battle against a determined enemy remained an open question. His mind was surely distracted this day. A few minutes after arriving on the field his younger brother, a lieutenant in the Royal Artillery, was felled by his gun— one of the few gunnery casualties during the opening cannonade.

Major General Alexander Leslie commanded Cornwallis's right wing below (or east) of the roadway. Immediately next to the road was Colonel Duncan McPherson's 2nd Battalion of Fraser Highlanders. The Hessian Regiment von Bose, dressed in their once resplendent blue uniforms and led by Lieutentant Colonel Johann Christian du Puy, extended the line to the right. The woods beyond their flank were less dense then those Webster would soon have to deal with. Lieutenant Colonel Norton's 1st Guards Battalion was also present and formed immediately in Leslie's rear. Leslie had served well as a brigadier general in the battles for New York, though his two regiments were sharply repulsed at White Plains when he led them forward in a conspicuously brave though exceptionally foolhardy assault. It was his soundly sleeping men Washington had slipped past on his way to attack Cornwallis's detachment at Princeton in early 1777. Leslie was rewarded for his careless handling of men and general lack of vigor with a major generalcy. Sir Clinton eventually despatched him in 1780 to the southern colonies to serve Cornwallis. It was Leslie who, at the head of twenty-five hundred men, had arrived in Cornwallis's camp the same time the disgraced Tarleton returned from his nadir known to history as Cowpens. Oddly, Cornwallis gave Leslie the position of distinction on the right side of the line—an honor more properly belonging to James Webster. Many expected much of Leslie this day, and many would be disappointed.

Rounding out the British order of battle was Banastre Tarleton's Legion of horse, which remained in column on the road in reserve. That was the extent of Cornwallis's army, some 1,950 men deep in enemy territory without hope of reinforcement or succor should a catastrophe befall them. Every Briton on the field had been up all the previous day, enjoyed little if any sleep, and had conducted a fitful march from before dawn until midday. Now they were about to go straight into battle with the sun directly over their heads. Food had not passed their lips for eighteen hours.

*   *   *

It was probably close to 2:00 P.M. or slightly later when Cornwallis decided to open the battle in earnest (he wrote in his report the time was "about half-an-hour past one"). In perfect precision Webster's front rank stepped out into the muddy fields and tramped toward Greene's breathless first line. Leslie's men moved forward a few minutes later. As if the tormenting sounds of beating drums and high-pitched fifes were not enough, the Highlanders added the uniquely desolate wail of Scottish bagpipes to the cacophony of sound filling the ears of hundreds of men already prepared to break and run should the chance offer itself. When the redcoats stepped off Captain Singleton, in charge of the two six-pound guns that had been blasting away from the bed of the New Garden Road—the same pieces that had killed General O'Hara's younger brother—limbered his pieces up and made for the rear. His counterpart's guns also fell silent. Exactly what happened next, and in what sequence, we shall never know for certain.

On the left of the road, James Webster's Fusiliers and 33rd Foot marched calmly ahead without incident. General Leslie's Highlanders and Hessians performed in similar fashion on the opposite side of the road. The cream of the Crown's colonial army continued on until they reached a spot about one hundred yards from the rail fence. Many of them must have wondered why the Americans had not yet broken and run for the rear as they had at Camden. Instead of running, however, the tattered militia delivered a ragged volley that dropped a respectable number of the enemy to the cold ground. Webster and Leslie pressed their regiments forward a short distance before halting to deliver a volley of their own. This time Carolinians fell to their own soil, but the blast seems not to have ripped apart the ranks as deeply as it might have. Perhaps the militia's lingering powder smoke had hindered their aim. No matter, it was now time for the bayonet. The veterans charged.

Sergeant Roger Lamb with the Welsh Fusiliers recalled that Webster guided his line forward "in excellent order in a smart run . . ." His men had closed about half the distance, Lamb continued, when suddenly the line shuddered to a halt on its own accord. The "whole [American] force had their arms presented and resting on a rail-fence and they were taking aim with nice precision." The British and Hessians could not believe their eyes. The militia had remained in place and were about to deliver a second volley at pointblank range. "At this awful period a general pause took place," remembered the Fusilier. "Both parties surveyed each other a moment with anxious suspense." Sensing an early crisis, Lieutenant Colonel Webster rode quickly in front of his left regiment and shouted, "with more than his usual commanding voice (which was well known to his Brigade), 'Come on, my brave Fusiliers!' These words operated like an inspiring voice."

And then the militia squeezed off their second round. It

An artist's depiction of the battle of Guilford Courthouse.

was a volley any professional soldier would have been proud to claim. Into this fire the Fusilier's "rushed forward . . . dreadful was the havoc on both sides. Amazing scene! What showers of mortal hail!" remembered Sergeant Lamb. The screaming leaden rounds ripped apart the Scotsmen advancing east of the road, remembered Captain Dugald Stuart, who wrote with some exaggeration that "One half of the Highlanders dropt on the spot." Another captain on the opposite side of the field with the Fusiliers called it "a most galling and destructive fire." The Americans thought so, too. One of Campbell's riflemen, who had taken up a position from which he could see the action clearly, recollected that the volley made the enemy lines look like "the scattering stalks of a wheat field, when the harvest man passed over it with his cradle." Neither the British nor the Hessians broke under the devastating fire. Instead, their surviving officers dressed ranks, bellowed out words of encouragement, and the men "rushed for ward amidst the enemy's fire. Dreadful was the havoc on both sides."

The North Carolinians had done their part as promised and now, finally, the time to retire had arrived. The fleetest of foot turned tail first and disappeared into the timber behind them. The rest followed, needing little inducement to send them on their way. Before long the entire center of the first American line had melted away. Guns were dropped, knapsacks and blankets pitched to the side, and anything that would lighten the load soon littered the wet ground.

William Richardson Davie had as much contempt for the militiamen and their officers as he did for his current administrative position. He did note, however, that "it is justice to the men to observe that they never were so wretchedly officered as they were that day." "Light-Horse Harry" Lee, who was always at the critical spot on every field, spurred his mount into the streaming mass of humanity and yelled without effect that if they did not stop he would run them down with his cavalry. His threats were ignored. General Edward Stevens, who led a brigade of Virginians in the second line showed great presence of mind by warning his men in advance that a deluge in the form of North Carolinians would soon be sweeping down upon them. Don't get caught up in the flood, he warned them, advising instead that they simply open ranks and let the frightened men pass. They did exactly that.

Nathanael Greene did not intend for the withdrawal of the first line to become a permanent retirement from the field. He knew well that Morgan's militia at Cowpens had re-formed to fight again, and this is certainly what he intended. Other than one small company on the far left, however, it is doubtful that one of them lifted so much as a rock the rest of the day. It is likely that this mistake in com-munication, if that is what it was, caused Greene to later write critically of their actions in his report of the battle. He them of firing too soon—some once, some twice, ome not at all. The field officers, he wrote, contradict- g Davie's claim, "did all they could to induce the men to stand their ground; but neither the advantages of the position, nor any other consideration could induce them to stay." Greene, however, is not a credible observer of this action because he was far to the rear with the line of Continentals and could not have seen any of it. Everything he wrote of he heard second or third hand. Captain Anthony Singleton, however, who was close by for much of the action, was quite taken with the North Carolinians's performance. "The militia," he remembered, "contrary to custom, behaved well for militia." The fight for the first line, however, was not yet at an end.

Although the militia had hightailed it into the woods, the veterans Greene had positioned on either flank remained firm. Their shooting was of the enfilading variety, a deadly mix of crossfire and accuracy that tumbled officers from their mounts and dropped foot soldiers to the ground. Clearly the British could not exploit their dearly purchased gains without ridding the field of these men.

Demonstrating that Camden was not a fluke, Webster spotted the problem quickly and issued directives to deal with it. Orders flew forth to the 33rd Foot to wheel to the left and face the threat while the light infantry company of the Guards and the small company of Jägers moved forward from the second line to assist them. The Jäger Korps, only thinly represented at Guilford by a small unit, had reached New York during the fighting for that city in 1776. The outfit was part of the Hesse-Kassel Army, dispatched to America by King George's German cousin and brother-in-law Frederich II. They were also unusual in that they carried rifles instead of smoothbore muskets. The Jägers often served as sharpshooters and were usually used as scouts and light troops. They were professionals to a man, and they responded immediately to orders that they change direction and tactics. In conjunction with the 33rd

Foot, the Germans advanced at a sharp angle into the woods in an attempt to come to grips with Washington's dismounted cavalry and the infantrymen of Kirkwood and Lynch. On the other side of the field, the Hessians of the von Bose Regiment did likewise, moving away from the road into the woods in an attempt to chase down and scatter Campbell's Virginians and Lee's horse and foot soldiers.

Unlike Nathanael Greene, Lord Cornwallis was commanding his men from a position immediately behind the action. He comprehended quickly what was happening and ordered up the rest of O'Hara's units and Lieutenant Norton's 1st Guards Battalion (to the right of the Hessians) to strengthen the attenuated line. Cornwallis's front west (left) of the road in Webster's sector was now held by the Jägers on the far left, followed on their right by the Guards and the 33rd Foot. All three were advancing into the woods against a largely unseen but deadly enemy. The rest of his line, apparently still facing forward, consisted of the Fusiliers, the Grenadier company of the Guards, and the 2nd Guards Battalion. General Leslie's sector, on the opposite side of the New Garden Road, faced a similar situation. Next to the roadway the ravaged Scotsmen of the 2nd Battalion of Fraser's Highlanders held the ground recently abandoned by the North Carolinians. Next to them, facing and fighting into the woods were the von Bose Hessians and Norton's First Guards Battalion. Tarleton, who itched to enter the action even as his crippled and bandaged hand throbbed in pain, advanced a short distance in column up the road behind McLeod's artillery. Tarleton had been told in no uncertain terms by Cornwallis "not to charge without positive orders, except to protect any of the corps from the most evident danger of being defeated." He was Cornwallis's sole reserve should any unforeseen disaster overtake the army.

The flanking Americans, meanwhile, conducted a masterful fighting retreat that slowly pulled apart Cornwallis's line and sucked the enemy deeper into the Carolina thickets. On Greene's right, Washington's cavalry and the riflemen under Kirkwood and Lynch fell back west and then north in a bitter fighting withdrawal to take their place on the right side of the second line of battle held by the Virginians. On the other flank, however, matters did not go according to plan. For reasons that remain unclear "Light-Horse Harry" Lee and Campbell's Virginians did not fall back to form on the left of the Virginia line as ordered. Instead, they withdrew north and east away from the main action. Lee, it will be recalled, by his own words was several hundred yards away from his command trying to stop the flight of the Carolinians. He may not have been able to get back to his legion before the thrust of the von Bose Hessians cut him off. If so, he probably had a devil of a time locating his men—which goes a long way in explaining his unusual performance that day. It would also be an embarrassing fact he would just as soon not publicly share. The deep-driving Germans and Norton's Guardsmen, meanwhile, vigorously pursued the North Carolinians, who waged a tree-to-tree bloodletting of the type so favored by the colonists. They would eventually remove themselves as far as one mile from the center of the action.

The anxious Virginians waiting in the second line never saw them again.

CHAPTER 5

THE BATTLE OF GUILFORD COURTHOUSE: THE SECOND LINE

"I was forced to ride over a British officer lying at the root of a tree. One of our soldiers gave him a dram as he was expiring, and bade him die like a brave man. How different this conduct from that of the barbarians he had commanded!"—Major St. George Tucker

THIRTY-SIX-YEAR-OLD EDWARD STEVENS listened with the ears of a veteran to the heavy combat waging unseen just 350 yards away. The artillery was no longer firing and the flood tide of battle seemed to be creeping steadily in his direction. He could not see much of anything. The woods held little greenery at this time of year, but the thick random sprinkling of tree trunks and brush limited visibility to no more than eighty yards. Stevens knew the faint screams and steady pattering of small arms were unnerving the twelve hundred men of the Virginia brigades waiting with him and his fellow brigadier, Robert Lawson, in the second line of defense. Most of these men were militia. They had never heard a shot fired in anger, though some of them were ex-Continentals who knew what to expect when the tidal wave of death rolled in their direction. All of them were scared. Frightened or not, General Stevens was determined his men would give a good account of themselves. He had watched in disgrace when his Virginians stampeded from the field at Camden like a frightened flock of geese. But seven months is a lifetime in war, and this day he resolved to hold them in place.

No accounts of what Stevens told his men immediately before the fighting have come down to us. Given his experience and personality, it is likely he walked along his line on the left wing (or east side) of the main road, pointing out to his men the advantages of their position. He would have alerted the young farmers and clerks to the fact that the entire line was stationed on a long wooded ridge that cut perpendicular across the New Garden Road. The enemy would have to advance up a slope to reach them. Almost every man had a tree or bush to shelter them. Their flanks, too, were secure because Greene had deployed riflemen and cavalry on either end of the first line. These veterans were even now falling back to protect their own flanks. If he was near his far left Stevens might have pointed out that very fact, for the firing in that direction indicated the presence of a running fight between Cornwallis's infantry and Lee's Legion and Campbell's riflemen. And don't forget the Continentals, he would have reminded them. They were not that far to the rear, where the ground fell away into the trees for about one hundred yards before breaking into an open bottom land cut by fallow fields and a shallow but muddy creek before sloping more steeply up to the plateau where the Regulars were impatiently waiting their turn.

Stevens knew the truth, however. There would be no help from the third-line defenders. His men were expendable, and their role was simply to hold as long as they could and take as many of the enemy with them as possible before surrender, retreat, or death.

*   *   *

Lord Cornwallis may have been temporarily taken aback by how well the North Carolina militia had stood and fought, but his judgment had again been proven correct.

Stand and volley once or twice and have at them with the bayonet, and they will break and run every time. And so they had once more. But a courier reached him a few minutes after the center of the first line had broken: a second line had been discovered a few hundred yards to the rear. Greene's army was not, in fact, on the run. No matter. He would soon enough have his second Camden. Without hesitating Cornwallis issued a flurry of orders to his subordinates to press their men forward and assault this so-called second line—just as Nathanael Greene had hoped he might.

On the left wing of the army Lieutenant Colonel Webster and General O'Hara took a few moments to reorganize their regiments as best they could before driving them deeper east and north into the timber. Exactly what position each unit held there in relation to its neighbor is unknown, but the high command structure was becoming confused. In all probability O'Hara's small troop of Jägers drove forward from a position on the far left, with the Light Infantry Guards company on their right and Webster's own 33rd Foot extending the line in the direction of the New Garden Road. Webster's other regiment, the Welsh Fusiliers (23rd Foot), fought closer to the road next to or among O'Hara's other two units, the Grenadier company and the 2nd Guards Battalion.

General Leslie's sector on the right side of Cornwallis's army was also beginning to creep into chaos. Hugging the roadway were the gallant Highlanders. Somewhere on their right was Norton's largely unbloodied 1st Guards Battalion, which was beginning to move well off the road and into the woods in an attempt to come to grips with the pesky American flankers. Colonel du Puy's Hessian Regiment von Bose was already long gone, slugging away with element of Campbell's riflemen and chasing after Lee's Legion. Tarleton's cavalry remained in reserve, though he had moved his horsemen forward several hundred yards to be closer to the action and more readily available when called up for duty. The forest had thus far made mounted pursuit impossible.

With all of Cornwallis's infantry up and advancing the battle took on a wholly different form. Behind them were the open fields of maneuver and volley, the fighting terrain owned the world over by the British army. In front and to their sides were the dark thickets and hidden ravines of the Carolina back country. It was into this quagmire they marched.

*   *   *

Nathanael Greene listened to the ebb and flow of the fighting from his third line. It was a curious command post for a man of his tactical ability and experience. Certainly messengers kept him informed of the battle's progress, but his remote position guaranteed that he could not directly influence affairs in real time. Why he willingly tossed that important card into the fire is unknown. Horatio Gates had made the same mistake at Camden; Greene seemed to be repeating it at Guilford Courthouse.

Edward Stevens's Virginians, meanwhile, held their fire and waited as they listened to the ominous bagpipes screeching their marching strain just out of sight. Soon the Highlanders would advance into range, and Stevens was ready to greet them. Small arms fire was already rippling through the woods to their right: Lawson's men were under attack. After what must have seemed a lifetime the Scotsmen stepped into range and Stevens ordered his men to unleash a volley and then load and fire as fast as they could. A hail of lead was returned, clipping twigs from trees and thudding into breasts and heads. Because of their angle of advance, elements of either Norton's Guards Battalion and/or du Puy's Hessians seem to have struck Stevens's line only lightly or not at all. Stevens, of course, knew none of this. For a time the battle seemed to be going well, with the redcoats unable to make much progress. It

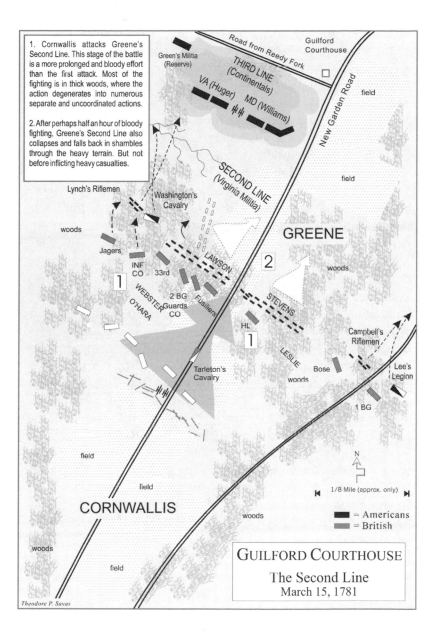

1. Cornwallis attacks Greene's Second Line. This stage of the battle is a more prolonged and bloody effort than the first attack. Most of the fighting is in thick woods, where the action degenerates into numerous separate and uncoordinated actions.

2. After perhaps half an hour of bloody fighting, Greene's Second Line also collapses and falls back in shambles through the heavy terrain. But not before inflicting heavy casualties.

Road from Reedy Fork

Guilford Courthouse

Green's Militia (Reserve)

THIRD LINE (Continentals)

VA (Huger)   MD (Williams)

New Garden Road

field

SECOND LINE (Virginia Militia)

field

Lynch's Riflemen

Washington's Cavalry

GREENE

woods

Jagers

INF CO   33rd

LAWSON

2

woods

1

WEBSTER   O'HARA

2 BG Guards CO

Fusiliers

STEVENS

HL

1

Campbell's Riflemen

Tarleton's Cavalry

LESLIE

Bose

woods

Lee's Legion

1 BG

field

field

N

1/8 Mile (approx. only)

CORNWALLIS

woods

= Americans
= British

GUILFORD COURTHOUSE
The Second Line
March 15, 1781

woods

field

Theodore P. Savas

was impossible for them to maintain their parade ground formations in the tangled forest, and so their headway was necessarily measured by the foot. Still, the steady pressure of the professional soldiers began to play on the nerves of the militia. The established action had now dissolved in bits and pieces, with small groups of men firing at one another and ducking for cover. But confidence began to build inside the general. His men were holding.

Exactly what took place on General Robert Lawson's front is open to much debate. His men were deployed along the same ridge line on the right (or east) side of the field, but were having a much harder time of it, even with Washington, Lynch, and Kirkwood in position on their far flank. Unbeknownst to Stevens, his fellow Virginians were being pressured by significantly heavier numbers that would soon coerce them into turning in a performance eerily reminiscent of Camden—or so some have alleged. The evidence seems to speak otherwise. Facing them were Cornwallis's finest, who tramped toward their position with bayonets pointing in their direction. The question that remains is how long they stood and fought.

No one disputes the fact that the left of Cornwallis's heavy line overlapped Lawson's right. The fighting there was especially intense, as Lynch's riflemen jockeyed with elements from Webster's and O'Hara's units for flanking positions to turn and throw the other back. The woods were so thick on this flank, remembered Cornwallis, that they rendered bayonets all but useless. Bullets were also flying thickly, and two of them struck General O'Hara, one in the thigh and another in his chest. The officer reeled in his saddle but managed to remain mounted. Bleeding profusely, O'Hara, who had witnessed several wars on three continents, insisted on remaining with his men, though he turned over active command to Lieutenant Colonel James Stuart of the 2nd Guards Battalion.

According to Sergeant Lamb of the Welsh (23rd) Fusiliers, "The second line of the enemy made a braver and stouter resistance than the first. Posted in the woods, and covering themselves with trees, they kept up for a considerable time a galling fire, which did great execution." A short distance in front of him Lamb caught a glimpse of an American officer running away. "[I] immediately darted after him, but he perceiving my intention to capture him, fled with the utmost speed." Lamb pursued and was gaining ground on the cowardly fellow when he spotted several small groups of Americans drawn up but a few yards distant. He had advanced far enough. "Seeing one of the guards among the slain, where I stood, I stopped and replenished my own pouch with the cartridges that remained in his; during the time I was thus employed, several shots were fired at me; but not one took effect."

By this time Cornwallis himself, whose magnificent charger had been shot and killed earlier in the fighting, was leading the attack against Lawson's stubborn Virginians. Lamb discovered him riding another mount through a thin spot in the forest. "His lordship was mounted on a dragoon's horse (his own had been shot) the saddle-bags were under the creature's belly, which much retarded his progress, owing to the vast quantity of underwood that was spread over the ground." Lamb remembered for the rest of his days the calm demeanor of "His Lordship, who was evidently unconscious of his danger." The sergeant had a better appreciation for the situation into which Cornwallis was about to ride, so he "laid hold of the bridle of his horse, and turned his head. I then mentioned to him, that if his Lordship had pursued the same direction, he would in a few moments have been surrounded by the enemy, and, perhaps, cut to pieces or captured." With the bridle in hand and trotting alongside the horse, Lamb guided both mount and general back to his regiment, "which was at that time drawn up in the skirt of the woods."

Though Lawson's men were performing better than expected, the British quickly gained the upper hand. Were it not for the survival of twenty-nine-year-old Bermuda native St. George Tucker and a letter he penned to his wife Fanny a few days after the battle, far less would be known of what transpired on the right front of Lawson's command immediately before it collapsed. Tucker was a learned observer who would live to become a successful lawyer, judge, writer, and inventor. But on March 15, 1781, he was a simple major of militia with an uncertain future in a most uncomfortable spot.

Tucker, who fought on the right front of Lawson's line, knew his wife would want a full account of the battle, but his limited view of the action prevented it. "I must candidly acknowledge myself totally incapable of doing so," he wrote her. He was able to tell her that the opening cannonade of "half an hour ushered in the battle," and that when it ceased, orders were given for a portion of Lawson's command "to advance and annoy the enemy's left flank. While we were advancing to execute this order, the British had advanced and, having turned the flank of Col. Mumford's regiment . . . we discovered them in our rear." Instant chaos was the result. "This threw the militia into such confusion that, without attending in the least to their officers who endeavored to halt them and make them face about and face the enemy, John Holcombe's regiment and ours instantly broke off without firing a single gun and dispersed like a flock of sheep frightened by dogs."

Tucker, with what he described as "infinite labor," managed to rally "about sixty or seventy of our men, and brought them to the charge." Others were not as successful. John Holcombe, who led a regiment on Tucker's left, "could not rally a man." Tucker and his handful of men "sustained an irregular kind of skirmishing with the British, and were once successful enough to drive a party for a very small distance." Dead and wounded were scattered about on the forest floor. As the fighting continued Tucker "was forced to ride over a British officer lying at the root of a tree. One of our soldiers gave him a dram as he was expiring, and bade him die like a brave man. How different this conduct from that of the barbarians he had commanded!" Unwilling to run, the major was "attempting to rally a party of regular troops when I received a wound in the small of my leg from a soldier, who, either from design or accident held his bayonet in such a direction that I could not possibly avoid it as I rode up to stop him from running away. The bayonet penetrated about an inch and a half between the bones of my leg. I felt no inconvenience from it for some hours, but have since been obliged to hobble with the assistance of a stick, or with some one to lead me."

By this time the heavy enemy pressure had bent back the right side of Lawson's line at nearly a right angle to its original position. Finding themselves suddenly close to the main road, many men used the opportunity to flee. The contorted line could not hold for long, and so it did not. Within a few minutes Greene's second line broke and fled, covered by Washington's troopers and knots of Virginia and Delaware riflemen. The latter men retired in good order and took up a position with the other Delaware company formed in the third line as part of the 1st Maryland Regiment.

On the other flank below the road Edward Stevens and his men were unaware of the disaster brewing on their distant right. They were still holding back the Highlanders and other unidentified groups of British foot when a musket ball slammed into the general's left thigh and broke his leg. A litter was brought up and he was carried from the field to the distant third line. His fall "accelerated not a little the retreat of his brigade," reported Lee. Stevens's Virginians were now fleeing en masse. Stevens would later receive Nathanael Greene's thanks and public praise for his conduct at Guilford Courthouse, and would go on to serve with distinction during the siege of Yorktown. The Culpeper native and one of the goats of Camden had wiped the slate of shame clean.

"Lawson's Brigade," wrote William Richardson Davie with a dollop of ridicule, "fought as illy as the No.

Monument on Greene's second line at Guilford Courthouse marking the spot where Brigadier General Edward Stevens was wounded.

Carolinians. The only difference was that they did not run entirely home." Greene had far kinder (and more accurate) words for the Virginians. "The Virginia militia gave the enemy a warm reception, and kept up a heavy fire for a long time," he wrote, "but being beat back, the action became general almost every where." Henry "Light-Horse Harry" Lee, himself a Virginian, agreed with Greene. "Noble was the stand of the Virginia militia; Stevens and Lawson, with their faithful brigades, contending for victory against the best officer in the British army."

The fight for the second line was over.

CHAPTER 6

Climax: The Third Line

"They fired at the same instant, and they appeared so near that the blazes from the muzzles of their guns seemed to meet."
—North Carolina militiaman Nathaniel Slade

NATHANAEL GREENE MUST HAVE BEEN nervous when he learned that his second line had given way, but he also had to be well pleased. His first line of militia had at least delivered a solid volley before breaking, and the Virginians had held their position for a quarter-hour or better. Both lines had inflicted substantial casualties on the enemy, though the North Carolinians had not regrouped on the flanks or in the rear as he had probably intended. Cornwallis's infantry had marched all morning and had been fully engaged for some time now. Professionals or not, surely they were becoming a bit disorganized and tired. His own Continentals, meanwhile, had remained stationary on the commanding ground of the third line, rested, fit, and ready for action. Washington's cavalry and the riflemen from Delaware and Virginia had fallen back and taken up a position on Greene's right, Singleton's guns had unlimbered on his extreme left, and large knots of Virginia militia were finally seen gathering by the courthouse buildings nearby. A few hundred yards in the right center distance a handful of scarlet uniformed mounted officers were spotted examining the Continental position. Within a few minutes

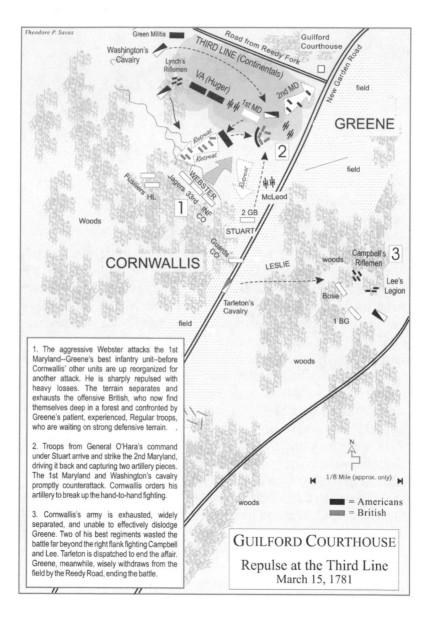

Theodore P. Savas

Green Militia

Washington's Cavalry

Lynch's Riflemen

THIRD LINE (Continentals)

Road from Reedy Fork

Guilford Courthouse

New Garden Road

field

VA (Huger)

1st MD

2nd MD

GREENE

Retreat

Retreat

2

field

WEBSTER

Fusiliers
HL

Jagers 33rd INF CO

Retreat

McLeod

1

2 GB

STUART

Woods

CORNWALLIS

Guards CO

LESLIE

woods

Campbell's Riflemen

3

Lee's Legion

Bose

Tarleton's Cavalry

1 BG

field

woods

woods

1. The aggressive Webster attacks the 1st Maryland--Greene's best infantry unit--before Cornwallis' other units are up reorganized for another attack. He is sharply repulsed with heavy losses. The terrain separates and exhausts the offensive British, who now find themselves deep in a forest and confronted by Greene's patient, experienced, Regular troops, who are waiting on strong defensive terrain.

2. Troops from General O'Hara's command under Stuart arrive and strike the 2nd Maryland, driving it back and capturing two artillery pieces. The 1st Maryland and Washington's cavalry promptly counterattack. Cornwallis orders his artillery to break up the hand-to-hand fighting.

3. Cornwallis's army is exhausted, widely separated, and unable to effectively dislodge Greene. Two of his best regiments wasted the battle far beyond the right flank fighting Campbell and Lee. Tarleton is dispatched to end the affair. Greene, meanwhile, wisely withdraws from the field by the Reedy Road, ending the battle.

N

1/8 Mile (approx. only)

◼ = Americans
▨ = British

GUILFORD COURTHOUSE

Repulse at the Third Line
March 15, 1781

drums and fifes were heard and lines of enemy infantry stepped through the distant tree line and walked slowly in their direction.

The climax of Guilford Courthouse was upon them.

*   *   *

Fitful outbursts of fighting could still be heard on the distant flanks of the second line when Lieutenant Colonel James Webster emerged from the suffocating smoky line of timber a good one hundred fifty yards or more west of the New Garden Road. His eyes beheld what one writer has described as a "natural amphitheater" that farmers had cleared of stumps and brush years earlier. The ground dropped away for a couple hundred yards to a low bottom land that looked to be creased by a small stream before sloping upward another one hundred and fifty yards to yet another American line of battle. This commanding position, complete with artillery, was not manned by militia. These men were Continentals, and Webster knew firsthand just how capable they were of standing their ground. Cornwallis was nowhere to be found. There was an important decision to be made.

Webster had three organizations with him: one company each of Jägers and light infantry of the Guards, and the regiment of the 33rd Foot—Cornwallis's former outfit. All three had taken casualties, but each was still battleworthy and ready and eager for action. The other regiments of the left wing were still deep inside the trees, either re-forming or exchanging fire with knots of stubborn Colonialists who did not yet recognize how badly they had been beaten. The longer he waited, Webster may have thought, the more survivors from the first two lines of battle could be gathered and placed into position to oppose his next advance. He had fought with Cornwallis long enough to know that his tactics demanded immediate and unforgiving assaults. Two such movements had broken through two American lines in a short time. A third would probably do the same. The courageous Webster instructed his officers to prepare for an advance. After his breakthrough at Camden, Webster had smartly wheeled around and engaged the right wing of Continentals still fighting on the far side of the field. He could have done something similar here, or at least helped mop up opposition, review the terrain, allow Cornwallis to reorganize his army, and then engage the Americans at full strength. The crush of time was not yet a factor, for many hours of daylight remained. In hindsight, it looks as though Webster's decision to attack without pause was hastily reached.

With his regiment of foot and pair of fighting companies aligned in good order Webster guided them to the assault, stepping smartly down the hillside in a northeasterly direction apparently aimed at the left center of the Continental line. It was an unpropitious avenue of advance, for he was moving directly against Greene's finest troops under Otho Williams—the valiant heroes of Cowpens and other fields. This portion of the line was held by Colonel Gunby's 1st Maryland (with Jacquett's rifle company and recently augmented by Kirkwood's riflemen, both of the Delaware Line), supported on their immediate right by a pair of cannons under Captain Finley. Webster's men crossed the twelve-foot-wide muddy stream, dressed ranks, and moved up the last slope. They were within one hundred feet when the calm Continentals squeezed their cold metal triggers, releasing a withering fire directly into their stunned faces. The left Virginia regiment of Huger's brigade also joined in the slaughter. British soldiers fell in heaps. One of the musketballs smacked into Webster's kneecap, a god-awful wound that shattered the bone and bled profusely. Somehow the gallant officer remained mounted. Either Williams or Gunby ordered the Marylanders to counterattack with the bayonet. The men from the middle colonies responded with a mighty yell, charging down the hill into Webster's dazed command. It was

The 1st Marylanders charge of the British is depicted in this painting by Frank Buffmire. *(NPS)*

the turn of the disciplined British infantry to play the role of untried militia. They simply could not stand in the face of such opposition and fell back in complete disorder. Gunby halted his men on the near side of the creek. "Recrossing a ravine in his rear," wrote one American officer, "Webster occupied an advantageous height, waiting for the approach of the rest of the [British] line."

Webster had attacked a prepared position uphill with a tired and heavily outnumbered force, his flanks wide open and without any reserve to follow up a breakthrough. In his battle report Cornwallis merely hinted at, but never directly mentioned, the failed onslaught. Perhaps he was trying to save the gravely wounded officer from embarrassment. Numerous American accounts of his assault exist, however, and it was surely delivered in a most imprudent fashion. Webster's hasty action demonstrated yet again the utter disregard with which Cornwallis and his officers held the Americans. The lessons learned from the bloodshed at Monmouth, Brandywine, and Cowpens had never taken root.

"Now was the critical moment of the battle," wrote historian Christopher Ward. Others writing since (and a few before) have echoed this observation. The basis for their excitement seems to rest upon the conclusion that Webster had attacked and been repulsed while the second line of Virginians were still heavily engaged with other British regiments (33rd Foot, 1st Guards Battalion, Grenadier company, and Fusiliers) west of the New Garden Road. The Hessians and Norton's 1st Guards Battalion at this time were far to the east of the road and engaged in a wasteful exchange with Lee's Legion and Campbell's riflemen. If all this were true, then Webster's bloody rebuff left Cornwallis's army strung out, widely separated, and extremely vulnerable to a determined counterattack. It is unlikely, however, that this was the situation immediately following Webster's defeat. Would that astute officer have slipped a veteran regiment and two experienced companies of foot through or past six hundred fighting Virginians and then leave them in his rear to attack a waiting line of American Regulars supported by four pieces of artillery? If his rapid advance had left such a large intact force behind him, it is much more likely he would have done as he had at Camden—turned and flanked them. Such a move would have easily bagged the lot of them. The evidence is much stronger that the Virginians had already evacuated their line and that the balance of Cornwallis's army was already nearing the open fields fronting the third line of battle when Webster launched his effort (perhaps while hoping for support) and was beaten back. We shall, of course, never know for sure. Nathanael Greene, meanwhile, let the moment pass without any decisive action on his part.

* * *

A brief lull in the battle ensued. The seriously wounded Webster refused to retire, choosing instead to remain on the field and regroup his bloodied and repulsed units. That decision, too, as events would soon prove, was the wrong one. His reverse had barely ended when Lieutenant Colonel James Stuart broke out of the woods on Webster's right, apparently at some point west of but near the main road. Whether the wounded O'Hara was with him is unclear. Stuart's own 2nd Guards Battalion was in tow, and the company of Grenadiers might have been as well. Stuart, it will be recalled, had assumed command of O'Hara's brigade after that officer had been wounded. Like Webster and so many others in Cornwallis's army, Stuart was aggressive to a fault. If he had spoken with Webster about the strength and fighting resolve of the Americans across the way, he might never have launched a similar forlorn hope. But the officers seem not to have shared a conversation. Neither was Cornwallis up to guide him. The Americans who had thrown back some of Cornwallis's finest had not yet regained their original position at the top of the plateau. Stuart was peering through the glasses of opportunity. Like Webster before him, he liked what he saw.

The 2nd Guards Battalion advanced in lock step, intent on delivering a bayonet attack to dislodge the far left of Greene's Continental line. The position was held by Ford's 2nd Maryland and Singleton's two guns, which he had withdrawn from the first line of battle and repositioned on the heights in anticipation of just such an event. A trick of the ground, however, coupled with a conveniently thick clump of trees shielded much of Stuart's advance from Gunby's re-forming 1st Maryland. Few if any of them knew or appreciated the extent of the developing threat against their neighboring regiment until the storm broke over them. The quick-moving British foot, silver bayonets thrust out before them, fell upon Ford's largely inexperienced Marylanders and Singleton's pair of field pieces with

Monument honoring the 1st Virginia Cavalry under Lt. Col. William Washington and the death of Captain Griffin Fauntleroy during the fight along Greene's third line of defense.

a mighty cheer. They had not even stopped to deliver a proper volley.

Ford's men panicked and fled to the rear, leaving Singleton's guns naked and subject to immediate capture. Once on top of the position Stuart's infantry discharged their muskets into the backs of the fleeing Continentals and promptly overran the artillery. The position—and perhaps the day—looked to be theirs. All Stuart needed was fresh troops to exploit his stunning breakthrough. His triumph would prove shortlived. Fresh troops were already on their way, but unfortunately for Stuart, they were Gunby's veteran Marylanders and mounted Colonialists in the form of Washington's cavalry.

Colonel Gunby was marching his 1st Maryland back up the slope perhaps one hundred and fifty yards away from the scene of Stuart's breakthrough when a courier pulled up his mount before his subordinate, Lieutenant Colonel John Howard, and informed him of the debacle. "I rode to

Colonel Gunby," Howard later recalled, "and gave him the information. He did not hesitate to order the regiment to face about." The men leveled their muskets "and gave them a well directed fire, and we then advanced and continued firing," wrote Howard. Stuart, too, had swung his line to face the enemy veterans and closed the distance. The opponents, veterans to a man, blasted away at one another at close range. A North Carolinian who had fought in Greene's first line earlier that afternoon observed the engagement from a position near the courthouse. The fighting "was terrific," he remembered, "for they fired at the same instant, and they appeared so near that the blazes from the muzzles of their guns seemed to meet." One of the British balls tumbled Colonel Gunby's horse to the ground, pinning the officer beneath it. Howard assumed control of the regiment and pressed the attack. More help was on the way.

After executing a fighting withdrawal to the second line held by the Virginians, Colonel William Washington had covered their retreat all the way back to the third line, where he had taken up a position somewhere on Greene's right flank. From that point his delight at Webster's bloody plight turned to shock when he watched Stuart's men steamroll up the hill and through the left end of the third line. The gallant officer gathered his men and galloped at full speed behind Stuart's trapped Guardsmen. With sabers drawn, they crashed into the British foot. Slashing swords hacked this way and that while others discharged pistols at pointblank range into the bright red uniforms. Fighting in one direction was one thing, but not even Stuart's professionals could hold their line and keep their heads with sabers slashing from the backs of Virginia chargers.

The decisive moment had arrived, and Howard seized it with a vengeance. While Washington's troopers were preparing to charge back through Stuart's Guardsmen, Howard ordered the 1st Maryland to attack with their bayonets. The two lines crashed together in a bloody hand-to-hand fight that Lieutenant Colonel Stuart could not possibly win. Captain John Smith of the 1st Maryland found Stuart in the melee and the pair squared off. The Briton thrust with his sword and missed by a whisker, the stab so close to Smith's torso that the hilt struck him in the chest. The move threw Stuart off balance, and when he tried to step backward he slipped on a patch of bloody gore and fell to one knee. A pair of Guardsmen rushed to his aid, but Smith finished the job with a mighty blow that cleaved the Englishman's head almost in half. The fallen officer's orderly tried to impale Smith on the point of a bayonet, but was struck down before he could do so. Another Guardsmen attempted a similar maneuver, but Smith ran him through with his blade. Finally, yet a third Guardsman leveled his musket from behind and sent a slug of lead into the back of Smith's head. He was feared dead, but had only suffered a bad contusion by a buckshot.

The bloody close-quarter fighting continued with the great mass of angry and screaming humanity moving ever so slowly west and south down the slope toward the British lines. It was at about this time, wrote one historian of the battle, that a Virginian riding with Washington's dragoons named Peter Francisco "cut down eleven men in succession with his broad sword." One of the Guardsmen pinned his leg to his horse with a bayonet. "Forbearing to strike, he assisted the assailant to draw his bayonet forth, when, with terrible force, he brought down his broadsword, and cleft the poor fellow's head to his shoulders." The story is embellished somewhat (Francisco claimed he killed only four men), but it accurately relates the intensity and barbarity of the action.

This was the scene that greeted Lord Cornwallis when he rode his dragoon's mount out into the open rim of the cleared ground a few hundred yards away. By now he had learned of Webster's repulse. To his astonishment that debacle was being followed up by a performance the likes of which he had never seen: one of the Crown's finest regiments was being slaughtered before his very eyes. If the

The dragoon Peter Francisco stands in his stirrups as he wields a five-foot broadsword in a wild melee against the British Guards.
(NPS)

affair was not broken up immediately and the American's bloodily chastised, there was no telling what the outcome of the day might be. Cornwallis also worried that the exhibition would dispirit the rest of his army, much of which was now watching the bloodletting. He would swiftly end the Guards's agony. If Cornwallis anguished over the decision he did so for only a few moments. Where was his Royal Artillery?

Lieutenant John McLeod, the Royal Artillery commander in charge of Cornwallis's three-pound guns at Guilford Courthouse, had been closely following the advance of the army all afternoon. When the cannonade with Singleton's pieces ended about 2:00 P.M., he had limbered his pieces and moved them north along the New Garden Road. Heavy timber had prevented their use against the second line manned by the Virginians, but the ground was now open and suitable for gunnery work. Cornwallis's order stunned the lieutenant, who though young had seen much of war: take your guns forward to the small hill near the ridge, unlimber them there, and flood the melee with grapeshot! Unlike solid cannon balls, which can be at least

This cavalry monument at Guilford Courthouse has plaques on its base which call particular attention to the achievements of Peter Francisco, Col. William Washington, and the Marquis of Britigny.

TO PETER FRANCISCO
A GIANT IN STATURE,
MIGHT AND COURAGE-WHO SLEW
IN THIS ENGAGEMENT ELEVEN OF THE
ENEMY WITH HIS OWN BROAD SWORD
RENDERING HIMSELF THEREBY PERHAPS THE MOST
FAMOUS PRIVATE SOLDIER OF THE REVOLUTIONARY WAR.

imprecisely aimed by qualified gunners, grapeshot could not. The smaller charge of iron balls exploded from the barrel like a giant shotgun and spread out in a pattern that ripped apart everything in its path. Cornwallis was ordering McLeod to fire into his own men. The wounded General O'Hara had been tracking the plight of his trapped men with no little anguish. When the order came he was lying on the roadside near Cornwallis. He begged him to reconsider the order, to no avail.

McLeod obeyed promptly and rode his guns forward along the road. When he reached an eminence (known today as Peter Francisco Hill) he unlimbered the pieces within musket range of the free-for-all and let loose, killing friend and foe alike. The grapeshot had the intended effect of breaking up the crowd, with the bloodied Guardsmen and colonials parting company. General O'Hara somehow managed to mount a horse and rally his stunned survivors, whom he guided rearward. For them, mercifully, the battle had effectively reached an end. Cornwallis's timely order may well have saved Stuart's regiment, which could not have continued resistance much longer.

The outcome of the day was still undecided. Tarleton may have put it best when he wrote after the war that "victory had alternately presided over each army." The battle was about to enter its final stage.

*　　*　　*

The odds were now leaning against Cornwallis and he knew it. His men were exhausted, hungry, bloodied, and scattered. Given the strategic situation he faced in the south, he had to win the day and decisively. Greene, however, had simply to avoid a decisive loss. With one eye on the retreating Guardsmen, Cornwallis kept the other on the units arriving behind him and to his left. It was time to take stock of what was available. In addition to the units with whom Webster had earlier attacked (the 33rd Foot, and two companies of Jägers and light infantry), Webster's "brave Fuziliers" had finally come up, as had the gallant Highlanders. The company of Grenadiers had lost every officer and had attached themselves to the cavalry and artillery. Both the von Bose Regiment of Hessians and Norton's 1st Guards Battalion were deep in the woods to the southeast chasing ghosts and riflemen. They would not see any more important action that day, and Cornwallis would sorely miss them. Thus far Tarleton's cavalry had played almost no role at all. Cornwallis decided to renew the action along the entire line.

The order to attack forthwith had probably already been passed along to the wounded Colonel Webster, who had re-formed his disorganized regiment and two companies and was even now leading them forward again on the left side of the field. His second attempt was not as decisively delivered. This time he struck the right center of the Continental line held by the re-formed 1st Maryland, Huger's pair of Virginia regiments, Kirkwood's Delaware elites, Lynch's riflemen, and Finley's artillery. Grossly outnumbered and again attacking uphill, Webster was easily driven back over the ravine a second time. He did not make the attempt again.

* * *

Nathanael Greene had spent the entire battle riding up and down his third line of Continentals. It is curious that few memoirs recall him during the height of the action there. Perhaps he was behind the Virginia regiments when first Webster and then Stuart struck the Maryland side of the line. The latter's attack, quite frankly, spooked him. "They . . . broke the second Maryland regiment and turned our left flank," he penned after the battle in his report, "got into the rear of the Virginia brigade, and appear[ed] to be gaining on our right, which would have encircled the whole of the continental troops, I thought it was most advisable to order a retreat." The general seems not to have considered throwing Huger's men into the fight to stabilize his left. "About this time Lieutenant Colonel Washington made a charge with the horse upon a part of the brigade of guards, and the first regiment of Marylanders, command- ed by Colonel Gunby and seconded by Lieutenant Colonel Howard, followed the horse with their bayonets; near the whole of the party [2nd Guards Battalion] fell a sacrifice." Not a hint of offensive consideration. Cornwallis was play- ing for an overwhelming victory; Greene was trying not to lose.

*   *   *

Webster had been thrown back again by the time Cornwallis's men were sufficiently organized to engage the strong American line. According to his report, General O'Hara himself led the decimated 2nd Guards Battalion and Grenadier company "to the charge with greatest alacrity," heading for the gap on the far left side of the Continental line where the 2nd Maryland had once stood. In reality, however, the "charge" was nothing more than a show of force. The American army was already withdraw- ing to the west along the Reedy Fork Road.

Greene had ordered the retreat about 4:00 P.M. A Virginia militia regiment under John Green was brought up and deployed to cover the vulnerable rear. The men were fresh, and had been held back for this very purpose. The with- drawal was "conducted with order and regularity," wrote one English eyewitness. The Rhode Islander probably gnashed his teeth when he learned that his artillery pieces would have to remain where they were; all of their horses had been shot down. Green's Virginians took a steady fire from the Fusiliers and Highlanders, who had advanced a short distance with some of Tarleton's cavalry, but when Cornwallis saw that they refused to yield at the sight of redcoats he ordered Tarleton to stop.

Banastre Tarleton, who had been chomping at the bit throughout the afternoon, was finally unleashed by Cornwallis to put an end to the sideshow being waged a mile to the southeast between Lee's Legion, Campbell's Colonial riflemen, du Puy's Hessians and the 1st Guards Battalion. "The pertinacity with which the rifle corps of Campbell and the legion infantry had maintained the battle on the enemy's right," explained Lee, "induced Lord Cornwallis to detach the British horse to that quarter. The contest had long been ebbing before this corps arrived, and Lieutenant Colonel Tarleton found only a few resolute marksmen in the rear of Campbell, who continued firing from tree to tree. The appearance of cavalry determined these brave fellows to retire and overtake their corps. Thus the battle terminated." It was not as simple as Lee portrayed it. From Campbell's perspective Lee's withdrawal was quite untimely, for it left he and his men at the mercy of Tarleton's dragoons, who charged and routed them from the field. "Ban the Butcher" only stopped when the ground became too rough for his horses to proceed any further. Whether Campbell ever forgave Lee or not is unknown.

The battle of Guilford Courthouse was now in the hands of the historians.

CHAPTER 7

AFTERMATH

"The more he is beaten the farther he advances in the end."
—British officer speaking of Nathanael Greene

"WE RETREATED IN GOOD ORDER to the Reedy Fork River, and crossed at the ford about 3 Miles from the field of Action, and there halted and drew up the Troops until we collected most of our Stragglers," Nathanael Greene informed his government. "We lost our Artillery and two Ammunition Waggons, the greater part of the Horses being killed before the retreat began, and it being impossible to move the pieces but along the great road."

The Grand Army of the South pressed on through the night with as much haste as its officers could wring from their exhausted men. The sun was well up the next day by the time they reached their old camp at Speedwell Ironworks on Troublesome Creek eighteen long miles away. There they remained, caring for the wounded, burying those who died after arrival, and preparing for a British attack that would never come.

Colonel Otho Williams, serving temporarily as Greene's adjutant general, compiled a list of casualty figures for the army. They were heavy. The Continentals, who had endured almost all of their fighting at the third line, suffered 57 killed, 111 wounded, and 161 missing. Some of the missing would show up eventually, but most of them had been wounded and were now in the hands of the British. More than 20 percent of the cream of Greene's army had been skimmed out of existence. Calculating militia losses was more problematic. According to Williams, they suffered 22 killed, 73 wounded, and 885 missing. These figures are, of course, woefully incomplete because the vast majority of the missing had simply up and gone home.

"Our Men are in good spirits and in perfect readiness for another field Day," Greene wrote in a report of the battle. "I only lament the loss of several valuable Officers who were killed and wounded in the Action." Among them were General Stevens, "shot through the thigh," and General Isaac Huger, "in the Hand." None of Greene's high ranking officers had been seriously injured.

The Americans may have abandoned the field, but Greene had done it on his terms with an army intact and ready to fight again. In exchange for a tactical defeat by the

This monument was erected in honor of Captain Arthur Forbis of the Guilford County militia. Captain Forbis was mortally wounded during the fighting at Guilford Courthouse.

narrowest of margins at the hands of the Crown's finest field officer, Greene gained an extraordinary strategic victory of a magnitude yet undefined. And he knew it. In a letter penned just seventy-two hours after the last shot was fired, Greene summed up the action to his friend Joseph Reed: "The battle was long, obstinate, and bloody. We were obliged to give up the ground and lost our artillery. But," he continued, "the enemy have been so soundly beaten that they dare not move towards us since the action, notwithstanding we lay within ten miles of him for two days. Except the ground and the artillery, they have gained no advantage; on the contrary, they are little short of being ruined."

After refitting his army and swelling his ranks with reinforcements, the indefatigable Nathanael Greene set off to conquer South Carolina. The next twenty months were filled with marching and fighting. He fought three significant engagements during this period—at Hobkirk's Hill (Camden), Ninety-Six, and Eutaw Springs—but tactically won not a single action. Including Guilford Courthouse, Greene fought four major battles during the Revolutionary War as an independent commander and lost them all. Each, however, was a strategic victory. After Guilford Courthouse, Cornwallis was no longer fit to take the field, and the same was true with the new British commander, Alexander Stuart, following the bloody action at Eutaw Springs. Greene's abilities baffled the best of Europe's professional men. One British soldier observed, "The more he is beaten the farther he advances in the end." A gifted tactician he was not, but in strategic abilities Nathanael Greene had not a single master.

*   *   *

Lord Cornwallis held the field at Guilford Courthouse. The rules of warfare allowed him to claim a tactical victory, but that is all he gained. His losses were exceedingly heavy.

Monument erected at Guilford Courthouse in honor of Lieutenant Colonel James Stuart of the 2nd Battalion of the Queen's Guards.

The magnificent fighting machine he had formed for battle that afternoon was now 28 percent smaller, with 93 killed, 413 wounded, and 26 missing. His prize Guards battalions had suffered slightly more than 50 percent casualties, most of these cleaved, literally, from Stuart's luckless but hard fighting 2nd Battalion.

Cornwallis had set out on the campaign trail to find and destroy Greene with some 3,300 men. When the sun set on March 15, 1781, he could field fewer than 1,450 bayonets. Not a single organization in his depleted army was field-ready. His officer corps had been decimated. Wounded in the leg, Lieutenant Colonel James Webster's condition worsened. He was strung in a litter between two horses and carried with the army when it moved out, but his condition rapidly deteriorated. Five officers died during or soon after that miserable journey ended. Webster was one of them. He lingered in agony for two weeks before passing on in a remote part of Bladen County, North Carolina. Cornwallis took the news hard. "I have lost my scabbard," he cried. The letter he would write Webster's father was a heartfelt tribute to the man Cornwallis most depended upon. Charles O'Hara was lost to the army for many weeks with serious wounds that would, twenty years hence, take his life. Dozens of lower ranking officers had also been killed or wounded.

Cornwallis's men must have cursed him the night after the battle when the cold rains, which "fell in torrents," opened on their unsheltered heads. "Near fifty of the wounded, sinking under their aggravated miseries, expired before the morning," wrote Charles Stedman. "The cries of the wounded and dying, who remained on the field of action during the night, exceed all description."

Cornwallis summed up his thoughts of the winter campaign two days after the battle of Guilford Courthouse. "The conduct and actions of the officers and soldiers that compose this little army will do more justice to their merit than I can by words," he began. "Their persevering intrepidity in action, their invincible patience in the hardships and fatigues of a march of above 600 miles in which they have forded several large rivers and numberless creeks, many of which would be reckoned large rivers in any other country in the world, without tents or covering against the climate and often without provisions, will sufficiently manifest their ardent zeal for the honour and interests of their Sovereign and their country."

His men surely deserved his kudos, but his vacuous prose did not address the true state of his situation. The Crown's strategic station in the south was far worse than it had been before the battle that Cornwallis should never have fought. His men were on the verge of starvation, the bulk of his wheeled vehicles had been burned together with their tents and baggage, and he was still many scores of miles from a safe logistical post. His foragers in the vicinity of Guilford Courthouse found slim pickings after the battle; the supplies of the neighborhood had been consumed by both armies. Many of the British soldiers went without food until the day following the battle. He had pushed his men through the cold and wet Carolina winter to the end of their endurance, and it was now time to seek rest, supplies, and reinforcements. Out of choices, he moved his beaten army to Bell's Mill on the Deep River on March 18, where he intended to obtain supplies for a longer march to Cross Creek on the Cape Fear River in Cumberland County, over one hundred miles to the southeast.

Before departing Bell's Mill, Cornwallis issued a proclamation informing the people of his "compleat victory obtained over the rebel forces on the 15th instant." He once again called on all the inhabitants to join the forces of the "legal and constitutional government." This proclamation was just as unsuccessful as the one he had issued a month earlier at Hillsboro. The battered and worn condition of the troops and the spectacle of the walking wounded followed by wagons and litters bearing more crippled and dying men did not inspire the sympathetic Loyalists of North or South Carolina to publicly show their support for the British government. Many assured Cornwallis they would join him when he returned to Hillsboro with reinforcements. But Cornwallis would never return. He later wrote bitterly of the trepidation displayed by the local Loyalists: "Many of the inhabitants rode into camp, shook me by the hand, said they were glad to see us, and to hear that we had beat Greene, and then rode home again; for I could not get one hundred men in all the regulator's country to stay with us, even as militia."

The lack of Loyalist enthusiasm was not the only disappointment awaiting Cornwallis. Major James Craig, commander of the British garrison at Wilmington, had been unable to set up a supply depot and outpost at Cross Creek. Craig had tried to inform Cornwallis, but his couri-

Cornwallis surrenders at Yorktown.

ers had been unable to get through before the British army was within a day of reaching the barren village. As Cornwallis noted, "not four days forage [was] within twenty miles." The British commander had no alternative but to march his weary army all the way down to Wilmington.

After resting his troops and reviewing the recent campaign Cornwallis made a fateful decision. He had had his fill of the Carolinas; other fields beckoned. The south could be abandoned, he argued, New York as well, and a grand battle fought for America in Virginia that would give the Crown back her rebellious colonies. Nathanael Greene had left the back door to Virginia open by invading deep into South Carolina. Cornwallis determined to march past him and seize the initiative in the middle colonies—where he had once been successful. His decision would eventually carry him north to Yorktown, Virginia.

One recent writer succinctly and correctly summarized Cornwallis's achievement at Guilford Courthouse thus: "Charles, 2nd Earl Cornwallis, had ruined his army."

Touring the Battlefield

The Guilford Battleground Company was incorporated in March of 1887 by the North Carolina General Assembly at the urging of Judge David Schenck. Thanks to the efforts of Schenck and his colleagues, a good portion of the land at Guilford Courthouse was purchased and saved from future development.

For thirty years, the Guilford Battleground Company worked to preserve and promote the battlefield. Visitors who came by foot, horse, or even train, rambled the field to view monuments the organization erected, heard speakers orate about the past, or enjoyed a small museum.

In 1917 the U.S. government created the Guilford Courthouse National Military Park. This was the first Revolutionary War battlefield so preserved by the Federal government. The Guilford Battleground Company transferred their assets to the government, and shortly thereafter went out of existence.

The Guilford Courthouse National Military Park was administered from 1917 until 1933 by the U.S War Department. In 1933, all battlefields under the jurisdiction of the War Department were transferred to the Department of the Interior. Guilford Courthouse, like other battlefields across the country, fell under the administration of the National Park Service, which still looks after the 220-acre park.

Facing the threat of urban sprawl and development, a group of concerned citizens banded together in the 1980s to reactivate the Guilford Battleground Company. This organ-

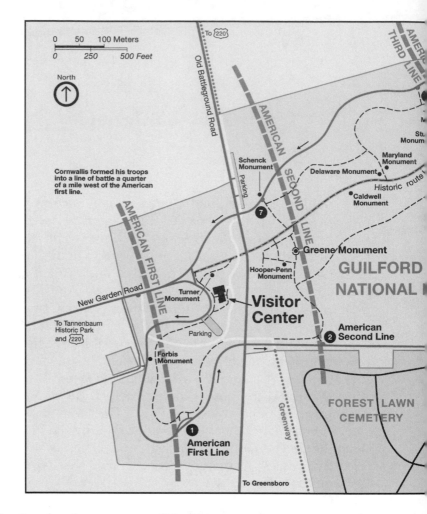

izaton has been responsible for preserving areas associated with the battle that do not fall under the jurisdiction of the National Park Service.

In 2001 much of the battlefield was designated as the Battle of Guilford Courthouse National Historic Landmark. This designation applies to land contained inside the bounds of the park, as well as other pertinent tracts in Tannenbaum Historic Park and Greensboro County Park.

The Guilford Battleground Company continues its work

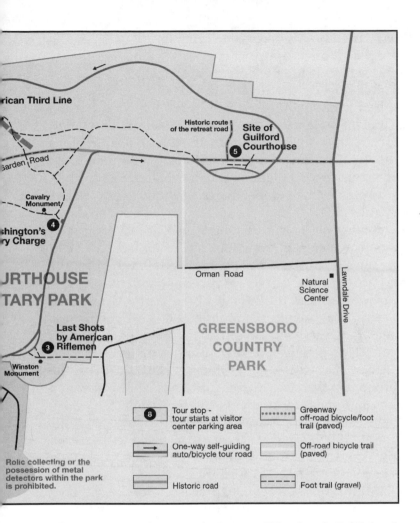

rican Third Line

Historic route
of the retreat road

Site of
Guilford
Courthouse
5

Garden Road

Cavalry
Monument

shington's
ry Charge
4

JRTHOUSE
TARY PARK

Orman Road

Natural
Science
Center

Lawndale Drive

Last Shots
by American
Riflemen
3

GREENSBORO
COUNTRY
PARK

Winston
Monument

8 Tour stop - tour starts at visitor center parking area	Greenway off-road bicycle/foot trail (paved)
→ One-way self-guiding auto/bicycle tour road	Off-road bicycle trail (paved)
Historic road	Foot trail (gravel)

Relic collecting or the
possession of metal
detectors within the park
is prohibited.

of preserving the Revolutionary War battlefield for future
generations. For more information about this organization,
write them at P.O. Box 39508, Greensboro, NC 27438.

*   *   *

When visiting the park, upon exiting the Visitor Center,
follow the signs leading to the park's Tour Stop 1. Here you
will find an interpretive sign calling attention to the open-

ing scenes of the battle on Greene's first line of defense. The first line was located approximately 150 yards to the west from this sign, outside the bounds of the park.

From this stop, return towards the Visitor Center but stay on the trail leading along the bed of the old New Garden Road. It is possible to traverse the entire length of the battlefield all the way to the former site of the Guilford Courthouse along this old road. For those with time to do so, it is recommended that one take this hike across the battlefield to gain a true perspective of how events played out in the battle.

For the purposes of this driving tour, follow the old road to the path which intersects just before crossing the Old Battleground Road. Turn right onto this trail, walk past the Visitor Center and return to the parking lot on the right.

In this walk around the outside of the Visitor Center, one will notice the numerous monuments and memorials standing along the way. These have been erected through the years to commemorate several individuals connected with either the battle of Guilford Courthouse or the Revolutionary War in North Carolina. For a detailed description of these monuments and the people they commemorate, visitors are encouraged to obtain a copy of the book, *The Monuments of Guilford Courthouse National Military Park* by Thomas E. Baker. The book is usually available for sale inside the Visitor Center.

Get back inside your vehicle, proceed left onto the one-way road, being careful to stay on the right lane which is designated for motor vehicles. The left lane has been set aside for bicycles and pedestrians.

At Tour Stop 2 is a parking area on the left of the road. Nearby is an informational display titled "Fragmented Attack." This discusses the broken nature of the terrain and how forces from the left of the American line retreated off through the thick woods and steep terrain toward the southeast away from the main body of the army.

Return to your auto, and continue along the park road to

Tour Stop 3, exercising extreme caution when crossing Old Battleground Road. At Tour Stop 3 is a parking area on the left. Informational displays here explain the fighting on Greene's second line of defense.

There is a hiking trail that leads through the woods along the Second Line of defense. Eventually the trail emerges into an open area with many monuments. Visible to the south across the grassy field is the Greene Monument. One of the most recognized landmarks on the battlefield; the monument erected in 1915 commemorates the service of General Nathanael Greene, commander of the American forces during the Southern Campaign. The monument, which cost $30,000.00, was sculpted by renowned sculptor Francis H. Parker.

A short distance south, standing in the edge of the woods, is another prominent monument. This one, known as the Hooper-Penn Monument, marks the graves of William Hooper and John Penn, two of the three North Carolinians who signed the Declaration of Independence.

This monument to General Nathanael Greene was dedicated in 1915.

The Hooper-Penn Monument where two of the three signers from North Carolina of the Declaration of Independence are buried.

Their bodies were moved to this site in 1894. The third signer, Joseph Hewes, died in Philadelphia during the Revolutionary War. His remains have not been located, and thus not returned to North Carolina.

While headed for the next stop, keep an eye open for the cemetery visible through a fence to the right, outside of the park's boundary. This is Forest Lawn Cemetery, whose well-manicured lawn stands a stark contrast to the woods and tangles that grew there in the 1700s, providing ample cover for the hit and run tactics of the Americans under Campbell and Lee.

As you pull into the parking area for Tour Stop 4 on the right side of the road, be on the lookout for two modest graves. Here lie the remains of Major Joseph Winston and Jesse Franklin. Both are veterans of this battle. Franklin became governor of North Carolina several years after the

Final resting place of Major Joseph Winston and Governor Jesse Franklin.

Monument to Major Joseph Winston and his Surry County militiamen.

war. The monument nearby honors Major Winston and his militiamen from Surry County who fought stubbornly alongside Campbell and Lee while many of their fellow militiamen ran for safety.

In order to completely understand the action on Greene's third line of defense, it is first beneficial to visit the tour stops 5 through 7. Next stop, Tour Stop 5, is located on the left side of the road. A short distance away is a large statue erected in 1909 to commemorate the cavalry charge of the dragoons under Lieutenant Colonel William Washington which brought the British army to the brink of defeat. The names of three horsemen who played prominent roles in the battle are inscribed on the monument: the Marquis of Britigny, Colonel Washington and Peter Francisco.

A plaque on the monument recounts the deeds of Francisco, who stood six feet six inches tall and weighed 260 pounds and was reported to have killed eleven British soldiers at Guilford Courthouse. A park service display nearby attempts to cast doubt on Francisco's feat, quoting the hero as stating that he only killed four men. It should be noted that he claimed to have killed four men, "in the presence of Col. Washington." Perhaps the others were slain while Washington was not present.

This display also puts forth the theory that the vale visible across the way is not the site of Greene's third line of defense, and thus not the site of the noted cavalry charge. The sign states, "Benefiting from historical information that has come to light since Schenck's time, park historians now have a different picture of what happened here. In 1781, the cleared area was significantly larger, extending toward the courthouse. Taking advantage of the terrain, the American third line was actually a ridgeline ¼ mile east near Tour Stop 6. By focusing on historically accurate terrain, you can better follow the chaotic battle action and its implications."

Thanks to modern archeological techniques and radar technology, park historians are quite certain that the

The trail traversing what is now believed to be the site of Greene's 3rd line of defense.

American Third Line is further to the east, and hope to clearly mark the line at a future day. Two cannon and a small interpretive sign mark the spot now.

Return to your car, and drive to the next stop on the tour, which is the parking area on the left side of the road. This is Tour Stop 6, which marks the site where the actual courthouse building stood during the fighting. There is no sign of the structure today, but a small building containing restrooms stands near the site. A trail leading north into the woods passes along the site which the park service now designates as the American Third Line.

Beyond this stop, the road bends around and heads west back towards the Visitor Center. The next stop will be a parking area on the left. This used to be the Tour Stop 6 commemorating the American Third Line. This is now, however, Tour Stop 7, and an interpretive sign, "The British Soldier at Guilford Courthouse," is located here.

A short distance to the south down the slope of the hill at Tour Stop 7 is a monument erected in honor of Lieutenant Colonel James Stuart of the 2nd Battalion of the Queen's Guards. He was killed in the fierce melee that occurred during the assault on the Continentals in the Third Line. A sword believed to have been Stuart's was found on this spot in 1866. The Guilford Battleground Company reasoned that this must be the spot where Stuart was killed, so the monument was placed here.

INDEX